Child Learning Through Child Play

Learning Activities for Two and Three Year Olds

Child Learning Through Child Play

Learning Activities for Two and Three Year Olds

Ira J. Gordon, Barry Guinagh,
and R. Emile Jester

with the assistance of

Diana Kronstadt, J. David Welch and Gary Weld

Illustrations by David Smiton & Rene Moncada

ST. MARTIN'S PRESS
New York

For information, write:
St. Martin's Press, Inc.
175 Fifth Ave., New York, N.Y. 10010
Manufactured in the United States of America
Library of Congress Catalog Card Number: 77-184555

AFFILIATED PUBLISHERS:
Macmillan & Company, Limited, London—
also at Bombay, Calcutta, Madras and Melbourne—
The Macmillan Company of Canada, Limited, Toronto

To Our Wives and Children: Esther L. Gordon, Bonnie D. and Gary D. Gordon; Susan E. Jester, Joseph Earl, Daniel Robert, and Byron Lee Jester; Becky Guinagh and Brady Guinagh.

Many of the materials in this book were developed and tested as a part of the "A Home Learning Center Approach to Early Stimulation" project, Ira J. Gordon, principal investigator, supported by Grant #5R)MHI6037-03, National Institute of Mental Health, U. S. Dept. of Health, Education and Welfare.

ACKNOWLEDGMENTS

Many people are responsible for the materials in this book in addition to the authors listed on the cover. We wish to acknowledge the Home Learning Center Directors who participated in not only the development of many of these ideas into this form but also testing these out with children and parents. They, and the families with which they work, deserve a special bow. Our Home Learning Center Directors were: Mrs. Rose M. Brown, Betty M. Ergle, Blondie M. Hickmon, Emogene H. Lee, Juanita M. Lee, Erma L. Mobley, Hattle Robinson, Pearlie M. Sanders, Susie M. Walters, Brenda J. Whitfield, Lyda M. Will, and Earther M. Wright. We also wish to acknowledge Mrs. Virginia Greenlee, who served as project secretary.

CONTENTS

WORD PLAY

DEVELOPING PHYSICAL COORDINATION

IMAGINATIVE PLAY

CREATIVE ACTIVITIES

INTRODUCTION

Research in psychological laboratories and in a variety of natural settings such as homes, day care centers, and other institutions has brought home clearly and sharply the basic importance of the first years of life in influencing the eventual intellectual and personal development of the child. Such knowledge either can lead to anxiety on the part of parents and other adults who have responsibility for caring for young children, or can be seen as a marvelous opportunity for playing vital and positive roles in helping young children grow. Further, most psychologists, pediatricians, and parents, as well as other adults interested in children, tend to agree on what they would like children to become. All would like children to be able to make their way in the world; able to deal effectively with people, with jobs, with social situations; and able to handle and use their own feelings well. Second, all would tend to agree that feeling competent is equally as important as being competent. Many of us know people who on the outside seem quite able, but who are really quite poorly adjusted because their own personal feelings are not in line with this outside view. Third, most would tend to agree that because we live in a complicated world, in which we have to know and get along with people from a variety of backgrounds, it is important that a child learn how to relate to all kinds of people but still preserve and develop his own individuality. Although these seem to be long-range goals, the success of a child in achieving them has its roots in these early childhood years. What we ask children to do, how we ask them to do it, what experiences we provide for them, how we react to their successes and failures, what behavior models we expect them to copy—all influence whether or not they will become competent, will see themselves as competent, and will develop a sense of security about themselves.

The years between two and four are special because so much happens in the child's use of speech and language. The child uses language not only to extend his intellectual development but also as a way of knowing and handling his feelings. Of special importance at this time is the way in which parents and other adults play with, work with, and care for him.

Many parents, and many other adults who are concerned with good day care facilities and good child development programs for young children, have instinctively felt that this is true. Lacking, however, were collections of specific suggestions for what parents and these other adults could do to provide the kinds of experiences for young children which are most likely to help children achieve these goals. Parents may say, "Yes, I know I should spend time with my child, but what exactly should I do?" Day care workers may say, "Yes, I know day care should be educational, but how do I make it that way?"

First, let's look briefly at how children of this age, two to four, learn. They can understand many more words than they can say. They are able to follow simple directions and enjoy showing off to adults that they can do it. This is especially true when the directions are gamelike and fun, rather than orders and commands.

They get their basic values and language from seeing and hearing what adults do and say, to them and around them. They acquire competence and self-confidence from their contacts not only with interested people but also by dealing with concrete materials: toys, blocks, paper, natural objects in their environment. They learn by doing things to these objects and seeing what happens. But this does not mean that simply providing materials and leaving them alone is always the most effective way. Although we recommend that a child be given ample time to play with materials in his own fashion, either before you show him something specific or after you have played with him, this by itself is not enough.

Since language and speech development are so rapid during this time, adults can assist in this development by surrounding the child with a "language envelope." Talk with him and to him about the game you are playing. Don't just order or demand that he say a particular word—such as, "Say 'ball' "—but use this and other words naturally as you play. Identify the object and the activity—"The ball is rolling"—or tell something about it—"That's a red ball." He will respond by first understanding the words and later using them in his own private play as well as in "conversation" with you. What we advocate is a natural use of language, not drill sessions.

Children learn by repetition. They enjoy and learn much from going back again and again to a favorite toy, a favorite book, a favorite puzzle, or a favorite set of materials such as blocks. Each time they play with them they see something new and grow. This means that children's learning during these years cannot be reduced to "lessons" which, once taught, can then be set aside and not practiced. The activities in this book are not "lessons" but experiences and opportunities for interaction with the child so that he is exposed to both the concrete materials and an interested adult who shows him interesting things to do and then encourages him to play on his own. What we urge is a balance between directed and "free play" activities.

Although it is true at all ages, it is especially true in these early years that the child's intellectual growth cannot be separated from his emotional development. Especially during these years, he approaches everything as a total being. When he is able to do something, he smiles and laughs or claps his hands. When he is frustrated or pushed or scolded because he cannot perform, or when he sees by himself that he cannot do what he is trying to do, the effect is not only in his brain but also in his tummy. As we will emphasize throughout the book, it is important that the adult always treat the child with a recognition that his thoughts and feelings are totally mixed. You cannot work on the development of his intellect without affecting his feelings about himself and his world. In your behavior toward the child it is important to examine what kind of attitude message you are giving him as you present him things to learn and do. Are you conveying by your tone of voice or gesture that you're disappointed in him? Do you stop the game because he does something different with it from what you'd planned? Or do you take delight and show it when he invents his own game, does particularly well, or stays with something far beyond the amount of time you thought he could be interested?

The purpose of this book is to provide specific, concrete, realistic learning opportunities for you to present to a child in a positive and loving fashion. This means that the atmosphere should be without pressure, but with enjoyment of the child's success, and also with a constant commitment to taking one's cue from the child. Their primary aim is to foster intellectual and language development. Included are suggestions for involving other children—older and younger family members, children in day care groups, or neighbors—so that the child will have opportunities for both a one-to-one relationship with an adult and interaction with other children.

Where can these materials be used? First, they can be used in the home by parents. We believe parents, especially in these early years, are the first and most important teachers of the child. Second, they can be used in family day care centers where there are small groups of children of differing ages. Third, they can be used in large-scale day care centers to provide the personal touch so necessary for adequate growth.

Although the separate games are written as suggestions to a parent, they are equally useful to day care workers and other adults in early childhood education programs. In those cases where children spend some time in the care of someone other than a parent, these materials can be used to stimulate group activities as well as individual ones. Each child, although he needs time alone with an adult, can also benefit greatly from playing with others. There is, obviously, a difference between a one-to-one adult-child relationship and the problems of group management. When the adult starts a game with one child, it is natural for others to become interested and try to get the adult to watch them or join the game themselves. Be prepared to have them enter the game as sharers, helpers, or separate players. For example, in a book game, each can point out pictures, help turn pages, or look in separate books. Many of the "muscle" activities are perfect for group play. "Imaginative play" is also easily turned into a child-to-child activity. "Toy telephone" is an example.

We developed these suggestions by using them in two kinds of settings: first, in the home by individual parents who had received demonstrations from home visitors who showed them the how and why; second, in small group settings of five children in a home in the care of two adults, neither of whom was a professional, but who had been specifically trained in their use. From these experiences we found that three-year-old children whose parents used these and the home activities suggested in BABY LEARNING THROUGH BABY PLAY: *A Parent's Guide for the First Two Years* (St. Martin's Press, 1970) were advanced over other children in their language and memory development. They also were able to relate to other children, work with strangers, and handle themselves with feelings of competence. We believe that most parents who read these materials can practice them on their own. Further, many parents will think up additional ideas as a result of reading these pages. Rather than seeing parents as people who should be bypassed in the education of their children, this book is dedicated to the principle that parents are teachers and can become even more effective teachers through using our suggestions. We believe that the home is an all-day learning center. Just as you can't divide activities up (except artificially), you can't turn learning on and off. As Dr. Ed Zigler, the Director of the Office of Child Development, said, "Learning is an inherent feature of being a human being." Therefore, the child learns from you all day long. He can learn positive things—such as feeling good about himself, using his brain and body—if you remember to set the stage. For example, eating provides many opportunities for learning not only language but also attitude and values and a sense of love and security. In reference to language, you can say, "Wow, look at Juan, he really chews his food. And Angela has already eaten her orange slices." You can describe the food, name the food, and talk about the forks, spoons, and bowls on the table.

Dinnertime can be a time when family traditions are developed. It is often the only time that all the family gets together in one place at the same time. Therefore, these times should be remembered as happy times, times when each child gets a chance to tell about his adventures. It can be a time for each family member to share his day. It should not be a time when parents tell children how bad they are or all the mistakes they make, or force-feed them or get into a battle of wills. Eating should be one of the great joys for children, not a time that he learns to dread.

A basic principle of human development is that no two children are alike. Even though you may find many books which will describe the typical two-year-old or the typical three-year-old, your own child or the children with whom you work never quite fit the description. While all children share some common characteristics, each is a special being who has his own path of growth. Therefore, the materials are not organized by chronological age, so that you cannot find here what to do for the twenty-seven-month-old child. The order in which these activities should be used depends very much on the child and on you. Even within a suggested activity, there is a range of difficulty. You may find your child is able to start right in, and move along. You may discover that, after he's started, you have to go back to some simpler approach, or let it go for a while and come back to it later. It may be that your child will want to stay at a part of an activity for a time before moving on. All these actions are natural. They remind us that these activities must be matched to the child's own rhythm, not the other way around. By careful observation, by trial and error, by seeing how your child responds and enjoys these games, you can decide how you will use them.

The book is divided into sections, each of which emphasizes one main type of game. However, since the young child learns with his whole body, every game is, to him, a mixture of muscle, thought, language, and feelings. Every game, in addition to its specific goal, contributes by its content and, most important, by the way *you* show the child your interest and enjoyment, to the combined goals of competence and self-confidence.

The sections are not arranged by age. There are games and ideas in each section that are useful to children of different ages. Some sorting and matching games, for example, will be just right for a two-year-old, and so will some of the "muscle" games. You might begin to use the book by taking an early game in each section, and see how your child enjoys it.

Remember what all the games have in common: you and your child, playing together, enjoying together, and growing together.

SORTING AND MATCHING GAMES

All of us deal with different kinds of problems each day. Some of these problems have only one solution. Others can be answered with a variety of responses. In this section we're going to discuss the child's early experiences with those problems that have one "correct" answer. Later we'll offer suggestions for helping him cope with the second kind of problem—where more than one solution is acceptable. There the emphasis will be on getting the child to develop his own solutions.

Researchers who have studied how young children learn have concluded that the child needs experience with objects that he can't change. He learns some basic facts from this. He learns that some objects can be grouped by their size or shape, or alternatively, that some objects can be arranged according to their use. He learns that objects he can hold and handle (three-dimensional) and pictures of these (two-dimensional) are related. The young child is interested in space and space relationships. He asks "What fits into what?" "What kinds of shapes look alike?" "How can I make things out of objects of different shapes?" "How do I learn the names for these shapes or objects so that I can tell somebody when I want to play with them?" The games in this section deal with regular shapes, such as triangles, rectangles, and circles, that he'll face later in math. They deal with groups of manufactured objects that he sees around the house and with nonmathematical shapes and pictures that have some "personality" to them, such as pictures of people and animals.

In all of these games you need to remember that they *are* games. Although there's usually one right answer, the child enjoys discovering this for himself rather than having someone else do it for him or tell him, "No, that's not it." Most of these games can be played by the child alone, but we suggest that in the beginning you play them with him, later providing him with the materials to carry on by himself.

Although the emphasis is on manipulating materials such as puzzles and boxes and pieces of wood and paper, we'll continually stress the importance of the conversation between you and the child. As we said in the Introduction, while the child works on these sorting and matching games, he's learning more than problem-solving. He's learning language, gaining self-confidence, and forming notions about his place in the world at large.

PROBLEM-SOLVING TOYS

There are many problem-solving toys, including such things as nesting boxes, a lock box, rock-a-stack, a sorting box, and puzzles. Most of these toys are self-correcting toys that only work one way, so the child must keep trying until he finds that way. With all of them, he has to manipulate objects with his hands and fingers. This strengthens his eye-hand coordination and develops his ability to solve problems—skills that will be needed later on in school. Another virtue of these problem-solving toys is that they don't lose their novelty quickly. Children play with them over and over again because they take time to master and because they are fun.

Nesting Boxes

The nesting boxes are five boxes, each one larger than the next. They work two ways. They fit one inside the other until they're all contained in the largest box, and when they're turned over, they stack on top of each other to make a tower.

Although this particular toy doesn't seem to have the long-term fascination for two- to three-year-olds that some of the other toys do, at first most children will be interested in the tricks the boxes can play on them. For example, if you place one of the smaller boxes inside a larger box, it looks like the smaller box has disappeared. Or you can turn the boxes over and say, "Now I'll take this big box and put it on top of this little box. Oops, it fell down over the other box." Then lift both boxes together and say, "Where'd that little box go? Do you see it?" Encourage the child to look until he finds the little box inside the big one (maybe with your help). Then ask, "How'd it get in there?"

The child should have some idea that the smaller box didn't really disappear, especially if he has played the shell game (see BABY LEARNING THROUGH BABY PLAY). Have him, by words and gestures, explain what happened. If he can't, show him, as though you were a magician exposing your trick, what went on. When he grasps it, he may want to "trick" you. Ask him if he'd like to, and laugh with him if it works. This will not only increase his understanding of the idea that little can fit into big (space relations) but will contribute to his grasp of the idea that objects still exist even when he can't see them. The idea of the permanence of objects is basic for later science learning.

Another use of the nesting boxes is to teach the child to grasp the concepts of big, small, bigger, and smaller. Start by using the largest and the smallest boxes. Gradually you can move to the in-between boxes and ask him to describe boxes where the difference isn't quite so clear. From there you can go to the three largest and show him the meaning of big, bigger, and biggest. He can also learn to arrange them in a row from smallest to largest, and begin to get the idea of "size place" and orderly arrangements by size.

Lock Box

The lock box is an ordinary wooden box with several different kinds of locking devices. It might have a game inside with which the child can play after he has opened the box, but this is really unnecessary since children usually prefer opening the box over and over again rather than playing with the game inside.

If you can't locate a lock box, make your own. They're easy to construct. Take any wooden box and simply add an ordinary chain lock, a screen-door latch, a bolt lock, and any other lock that you can find in a hardware store.

In a group setting, spend a few minutes with each child helping him undo each of the locks. After a while, let him play with the box by himself, helping him only when he asks for it. This is a toy with which one child will spend a lot of time, enabling you to give individual attention to another child, if need be.

Rock-A-Stack

The rock-a-stack consists of a number of rings (the number varies) that fit over a pole anchored in a rocking base. The pole is larger at the bottom than at the top, so that it's self-correcting. Only the largest ring will go all

the way down to the bottom. When you show the child the rock-a-stack, say, "All of the rings fit over this pole. First, we dump all of the rings off of the stack. Now they're all over the floor. How are we going to get them back on the stack? Can you put them back on? You can? Good!" At this point the child probably won't care if the rings are on the stack correctly or not. He'll have a good time simply trying to get all of the rings on the stack. When you decide that it's time for him to learn how to assemble the stack correctly, show him how to use his hands and eyes to judge if the ring is in the proper place. Don't do it for him! Describe for him what's happening—"The orange one didn't go all the way down, I wonder which one will—what one will you try now?" Let the child learn from the toy, with your words as "background music" but not commands.

Put on a ring and then both of you decide if it's on correctly. Ask the child if it's all the way down. Remember that you're teaching a two-to-three year old and that this isn't an easy thing to learn and might take a while. As in all these games, try to convey new things in such a natural way that they come about through play and not through a "hard-headed" instructional session.

Sorting Box

The sorting box is usually made of wood. It looks very much like an ordinary box except that the top has several holes cut in it, each a different shape. Wooden blocks, cut to the shape of the holes, are carried inside. The object of the sorting box is to teach the child to make distinctions based on shape.

This is a toy that needs no introduction to the child. You can just put it down, empty it out, and let the child play with it. Some children will pick out a favorite shape and put it into the box over and over. After a while, if you notice this happening, you can remove that piece from the box, which will require the child to move on to another piece.

Teaching the sorting box is best approached in a gamelike way. One way is to join the child and put blocks into the holes. Ask him if he knows where a block goes. Encourage him to point to the hole. If it doesn't go in, say, "Hmm, did it go in?" When he says or indicates No, ask, "Can you help me?" If you can get the child to try each piece in each hole, he'll soon learn that a particular piece goes in a particular hole. You may have difficulty in getting him to do this, since the tendency of many children is to try a block in one hole, then—if it doesn't go in—throw it away and try another block. But if you succeed you will have taught him to solve a problem through trial and error—an important lesson.

In a group setting, several children can use the sorting box simultaneously, and the older ones can help the younger ones. The older children will often be more patient (if they have been shown patience in their learning) than many adults.

To vary the game, have the children take turns, each child trying one shape. You can start it and then let the children take over. You'd be surprised how often children can manage group games—even when they're this young—if there's a lot of motor activity in the game and they enjoy it.

Usually, the sorting box comes with two blocks of each shape. You can use these to play matching games with the child. Take one block of each shape and put the others in a pile in front of him. Say, "I have a block and you have one just like it. Can you find it?" Sometimes it's helpful to describe to the child the block you have. Talk about its sides, its shape—even give it a name if you like. Encourage the child to examine the block carefully before he tries to pick its mate. If he guesses right, say "Good boy, you really know

your shapes." If he's unable to find the matching block, say "Uh oh, you didn't get it that time. I bet you will this time." Give the child a little help if he needs it by reducing the number of choices and by talking to him throughout the game. In any case, don't overdo it. If he gets frustrated or tired of the game, move on to something else and come back to matching later.

Puzzles

Puzzles are probably the easiest toys to find on the market and their variety is virtually limitless. Wooden or hard plastic puzzles are better than rubber ones; they seem to last longer and are easier to handle. Usually, the easiest puzzle is one with one piece cut out in some shape like a truck, a cow, or a tool. These puzzles are very much like the sorting box, since they involve matching a shape to its cutout image. Children like them and have fun with them. After a while, you can introduce other puzzles that have two or more pieces. Try to get a puzzle that breaks up in recognizable shapes—for example, a puzzle of a truck that separates the truck by tires, truck bed, door, hood, and so on. It's easier to put together, and it allows you to teach the child the name of each part.

The child will play with puzzles over and over. He'll return again and again to a puzzle that he has mastered and you think is too simple for him. We tend to forget that children enjoy success as much as we do, and going back to do something we know we can do is very reassuring. Practicing on known things lays the foundation for learning new things. So let your child practice on simple puzzles even after he has mastered more complex ones.

BLOCKS AND BLOCK PLAY

Of all toys, blocks seem to hold children's attention the most. Perhaps it's because there are so many things they can do with them. Blocks can be used for building, hauling, cooking, driving, flying, or floating—in fact, for just about anything.

Blocks are included in this section because of their uniform shapes and because they lend themselves to a variety of sorting and matching tasks. They also can be used for imaginative and creative play.

Stacking

At first your child may want to line up the blocks like a train, a preliminary step to stacking which is probably the most elementary block game for two- to three-year-olds. If you begin stacking, it's likely that the child will help you. Don't be concerned if the stacks aren't very neat or straight. If they aren't straight they'll fall down, and the child will enjoy the falling as much as the building.

Stacking leads into real building. While you're stacking one day, say, "I'm going to build a house. Does anybody want to help? I'm going to build my wall very high. I'll build my wall here and you build your wall there. Oh, you want to help build my wall? (Children don't want to build their own walls very often.) O.K., first I'll put a block on and then you put a block on. There's mine. And there's yours. Good boy! This is going to be a fine house."

Blocks are ideal for group play. Children can cooperate in building houses, roads, castles, and other structures. They can then use the buildings for other types of games.

In a day care center problems may arise out of group use of blocks. The caregiver should use these situations as chances to teach social rules. Some children may want to leave their creations standing when the day is over. Often this is not possible. Other children may want to "pirate" blocks from their classmates for their own use.

In the home, the parents should recognize the child's pride in what he builds and, if possible, let it stand, even if it may be slightly inconvenient.

Block Play

The next games all use blocks to increase skill in sorting. Set out six or eight blocks of two different sizes. Let the child play with them in any fashion he wants. He can build a tower, lean the blocks against each other, or make a road. After he has handled the blocks for a while, take one of each size and place one on top of the other.

Ask the child, by pointing to a particular block, to give you a little one and then a big one. Keep doing this until you have used all the blocks to make something. You don't have to use them in any particular order, but keep emphasizing to the child the differences in sizes.

Next, using the same set of blocks, jumble them all together in a pile, take one, and tell the child, "Give me another one that's this size or looks like this." Explain to him what "same size" means by running your hand and his around the edges. Have him look at the block and turn it at different angles.

When he hands you another block, let him compare the two by holding them together and matching edges. Ask again, "Is it just like this? Are these alike?" If he says Yes, put them together in the same pile. Then take the other-size block and do the same thing. Continue until all the blocks have been piled.

If the child doesn't understand what you mean by "alike" or "just like this," try using other words he knows to get across the same idea. You might have him place the two blocks together and handle them so that he's using his eyes and his hands to understand the idea of "sameness," even though he doesn't understand the words. Call on your own creativity here, finding ways to get the child to understand what "alike" means. In any case, if he isn't having fun don't force him to learn. You can reduce his frustration by letting him return to playing with the blocks as he wishes.

In the last game we used size as the basis for distinguishing between different blocks. Here, we'll use color.

Give him two sets of blocks—some of them red, some of them blue. (Make sure they're the same size.) At first, don't use more than two colors. Let him play with the blocks in his usual way. Then join him on the floor. Pick a block and ask him to give you one that looks like it. Blocks of the same color should go in the same pile, as blocks of the same size went in the same pile in the first game.

If the child enjoys this activity, you may want to add a third-color block and so on.

Keep in mind that children this age pay attention to only one fact about an object at a time. Later on you might want the child to recognize the shape, size, and color of a block all at once. But initially, it's best to stick to one characteristic.

Children of this age (and indeed up to the age of four or five) can't name colors although they do recognize color differences. You should use the names red and blue but most likely he will not name the blocks by color. Nor can you expect him to give you the right-colored block when you ask him for it. There will be enough time for him to use the name of a color later on. Here we just want him to use the fact of color.

SORTING TWO SETS OF OBJECTS

A basic skill important in the child's intellectual development is the ability to organize things into groups. Sorting games are excellent for developing this skill. In this section we talk about two kinds of sorting games: one that helps teach sorting by appearance, the other, sorting by function or use.

When showing two- to three-year-olds how to sort, it's usually best to begin with only two different kinds of objects. After this is mastered, go on to three, four, and even five different kinds.

The only materials needed for this game are the objects to be sorted and two boxes to put them in. Any two types of objects will do: buttons and spools, blocks and marbles, or even paper strips and beads.

Spread the pieces in front of the child and say, "Here are some buttons and here are some spools." Place a box on either side of him. Show the child one box and say, "Help me put all the buttons in this box and all the spools in that other box." If he makes a mistake, say something like "Oops, does that go there? Does it look like the others?" Help him see his mistake—don't just tell him or put the misplaced object in the proper box yourself.

After all of the buttons and spools are in the correct boxes, dump them all out into a pile and start again. Keep on doing this until the child wants to stop or wants to increase the number of things to sort. This is a good game to play every day. You can vary it by making the objects harder and harder to sort.

A harder version of the game is to sort by use instead of appearance. Your groups of objects may include "things to eat with" and "toys to play with." It may be hard for the child to grasp this distinction at first. He may want to play with forks and spoons, for example. In his mind, these may not be separate groups. He should catch on after a while, however, especially after he comes to associate spoons and forks with eating, an activity he'll recognize as different from playing games. Getting the child to sort by use or function has innumerable possibilities as a game, and you probably will want to add your own variations.

MATCHING IDENTICAL OBJECTS

An important part of the growing process is learning to identify and sort objects. To do this quickly and accurately it's necessary to recognize how things are alike and how they are different. This helps the child learn to match identical objects. It also helps him learn how to arrange things in an orderly way.

The ability to match and arrange has many benefits. One immediate gain would be that the child might learn to help sort things around the house. A long-range benefit is the ability to organize, important not only in dealing with school subjects—such as math or composition—but also in managing one's daily life.

You'll need pairs of identical objects, such as two soda bottles, two teacups, two bottlecaps, two clothespins, or two teaspoons. Start with only three or four pairs so you don't confuse the child.

Before you begin the game, find a clear space on which to work—a whole tabletop, for example. Put the three or four pairs of objects on the table. It might be easier for the child if the objects are arranged in pairs when you start. Then say, "Look! Here are two things *just alike!*"

When you do this, sound excited. This will help focus the child's attention.

Next, separate the pairs so that they stand out very clearly as groups or pairs. Again say excitedly, "Here are two things that are *just alike!*"

After you've done this, mix the objects up. Then pick them up one by one and ask the child, "Can you find one just like this?" If he has trouble, don't keep asking him over and over; help him find the mate. While you're helping him, talk about what you're doing. For example, if you pick up a clothespin and the child isn't able to find another like it, pick up the other clothespin and say, "See, *this* is just like the clothespin here." (Point to the other clothespin or hold it up so he can compare the two.) You might then say, "They're both made of wood," or "They're both the same color," or "They both have springs." When talking about identical objects, you should use the words "same" and "alike" as well as words describing the objects.

You can play this game almost anywhere or any time, whenever you notice that two things are alike.

MATCHING OBJECTS AND PICTURES

It is difficult for young children to understand the relationship between a real object and its picture. One of the facts discovered about some children who were having trouble learning in the early school grades was that they lacked the ability (because of lack of experience) to grasp the idea that not only could a picture and the object be called by the same name, but that the picture represented the object. This is a basic idea for learning to read—that the symbols on the page mean something.

This section has games that will give a child practice matching objects with their pictures. You can begin by drawing or tracing an outline of familiar objects that might be found around the home, such as a popsicle stick, a block, a leaf, possibly a pair of scissors or a knife. Or you may want to start by tracing an outline of your hand or your child's. Let him watch you do this. Encourage him to help you by letting him hold the object in place or even draw the line.

While you are drawing the outline, talk to him, describing what you're doing. Say, "Help me draw a picture of a leaf. You hold the leaf and I'll draw all around the edges. There, I'm all finished! What do you think is underneath? Let's see."

Talk about similarities between the picture and the leaf. Say, "Look, the leaf has a sharp point up on top and so does the picture." As a variation, let the child select objects to draw. After you've drawn several different objects, make a game of matching the object with its picture.

Say, "I'm going to put the leaf on its picture. See? Now you put something on its picture. Good boy!" Don't worry too much about lining the object up on its picture. The important thing is that the child recognize the similarity between the two.

There are several ways to vary the game and still keep it interesting. Cut pictures from magazines or coloring books and let the child match the objects with these. Then reverse this and give the child an object and have him find it in the magazine. You can also have the child match pictures with other pictures. For example, if you have two pictures of plates, see if he can match them. The pictures don't necessarily have to be identical, but they should be similar. Pictures of animals such as dogs, horses, or cows are good for this game.

Remember to describe the pictures and objects with which you're playing so the child will learn something about the objects themselves.

CARDBOARD CUTUPS

The recognition of simple patterns and designs forms the basis of many play and school activities, ranging from jigsaw puzzles to reading. This next set of games gives the child experience with a variety of patterns and also gives him a chance to make some of his own. Along with making his own designs, the child also gets practice manipulating objects with his fingers and hands.

You'll need a large piece of cardboard—about two feet by three feet would be good; six pieces of cardboard about four inches square—they can be a little bigger or smaller, but they must be *square;* a pair of scissors; and some crayons.

To complete your set of materials, cut two of the small squares exactly in the middle, so that you have four rectangles. Then, cut two of the other small squares along the diagonal, so that you have four triangles. Now, you have two "sets", each composed of two triangles, two rectangles, and one square. Give one set to the child.

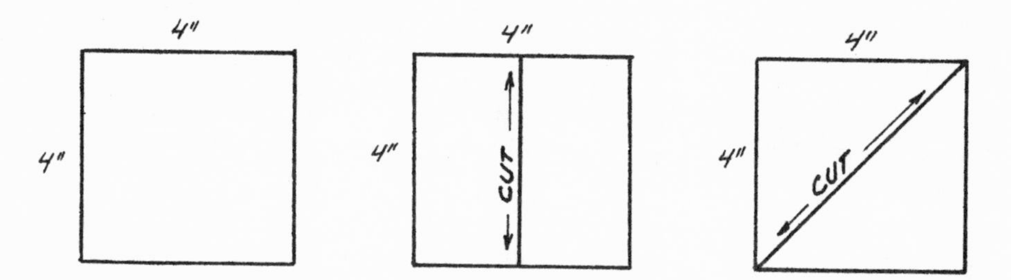

Now, using a crayon and the shapes you have just cut, draw some of the designs shown below on the large cardboard sheet.

Place one of the cutouts within its outline on the big sheet, then encourage the child to do the same: "Now, *you* match a piece with its outline." Try to work on only one or two designs at a time so the child doesn't become confused.

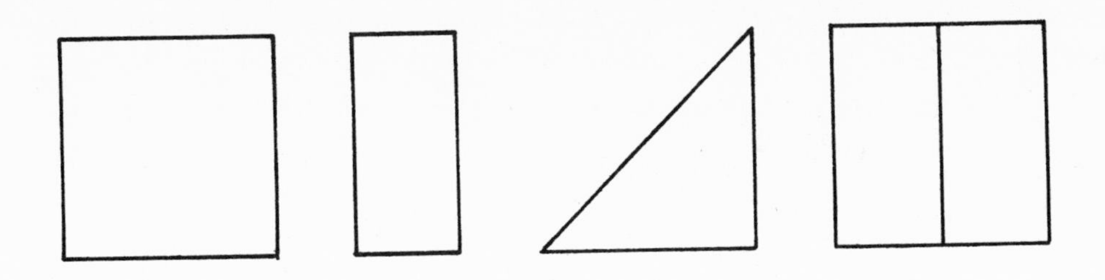

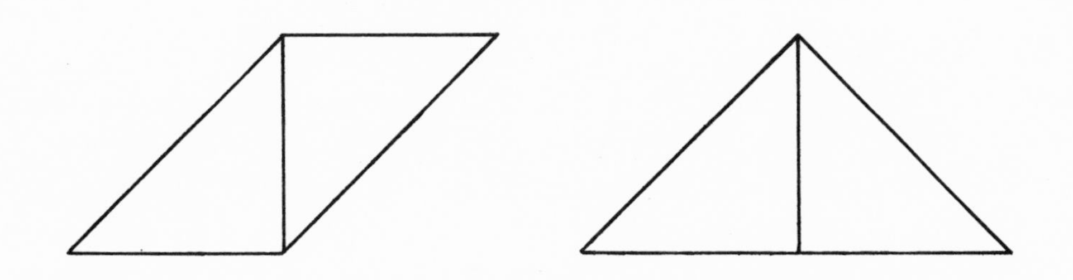

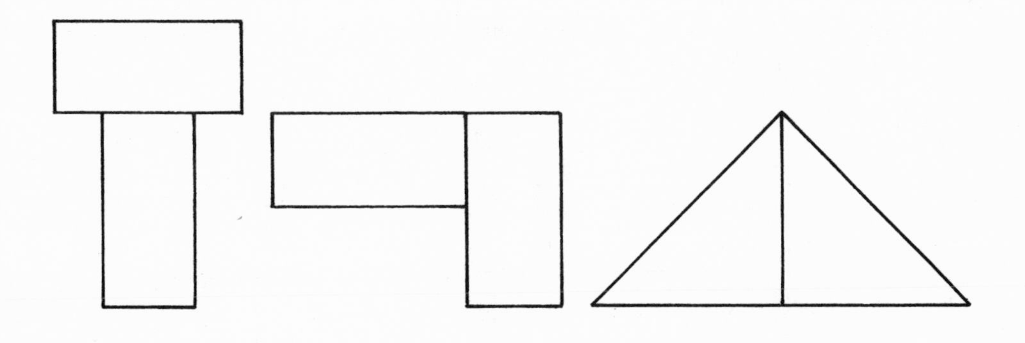

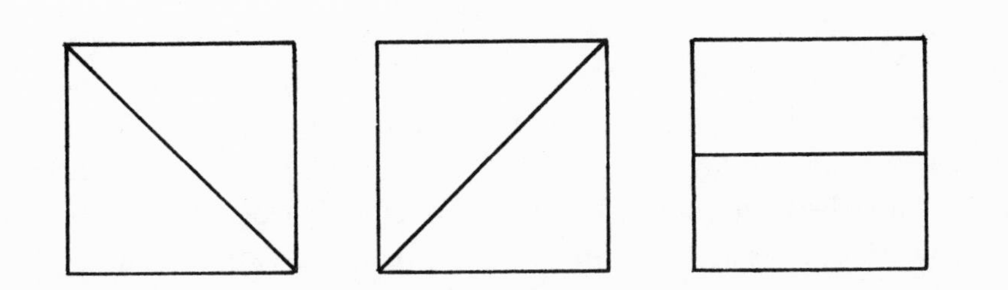

After a design is completed, ask him if he'd like to color it (either the pieces or the outline). If he doesn't, that's O.K. Just draw more designs. Whenever you give a child a choice it's very important that you accept it. Otherwise, he'll soon learn that his choice really doesn't matter.

Here's something else to do. Turn the large sheet over so the designs don't show. Take two or three of the small cardboard pieces and arrange them in a design that looks like a familiar object. Here are a few of the things you can make with these pieces:

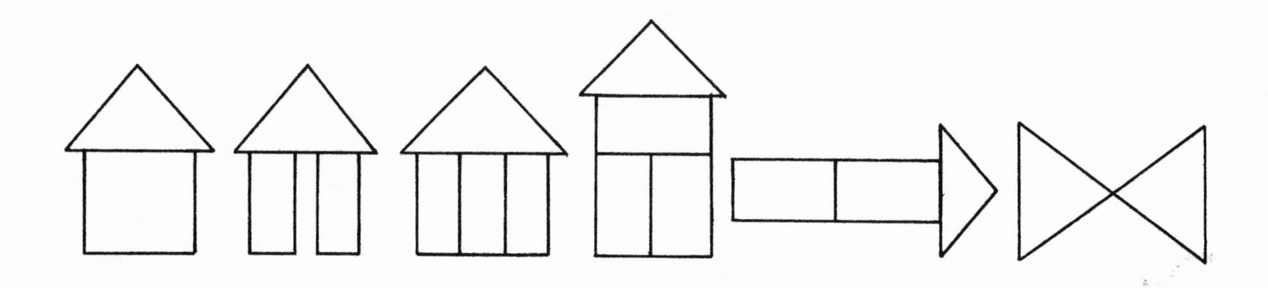

Now ask the child to do the same thing with some of his pieces. This game is a little harder, since there are no lines to guide him. He's got to make repeated comparisons with the model you build.

This type of activity gives the child practice in seeing the differences and similarities between things. If you find what he has done differs from your model and he doesn't see the difference between the two, encourage him to look again. Point out the difference. But don't make him change his.

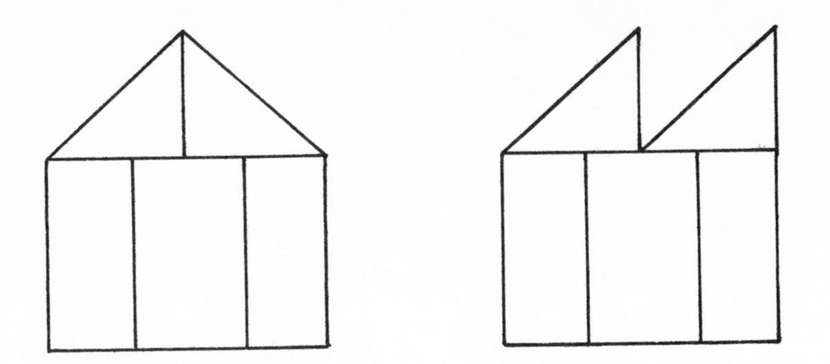

"See, Johnny, this triangle points the other way on my house. You've made a different type of house." Don't demand conformity. The important thing is that he see the difference, not that he copy everything you make.

After you've played this way for a while, reverse roles. (You can and should do this in most of your teaching games.) Let the child build a model for you to copy. Occasionally make your shape different from his, let him point the difference out to you. In this way, he'll not only be getting practice in distinguishing between shapes, but will probably feel proud at being able to correct you.

In many ways, this game is a simpler form of blocks. It teaches the child how to arrange different shapes to make whatever he wants, and it gives him experience building a whole out of individual parts.

SHAPES ON CARDS

A child's ability to see the differences in shapes is a forerunner of his ability to learn the letters of the alphabet and to read. Here's another activity to help him become familiar with different shapes. You'll need about six cards with the shapes cut out. Here's how you can make them:

Cut cardboard, or heavy paper into six strips. Each strip should be about ten inches long and two inches wide.

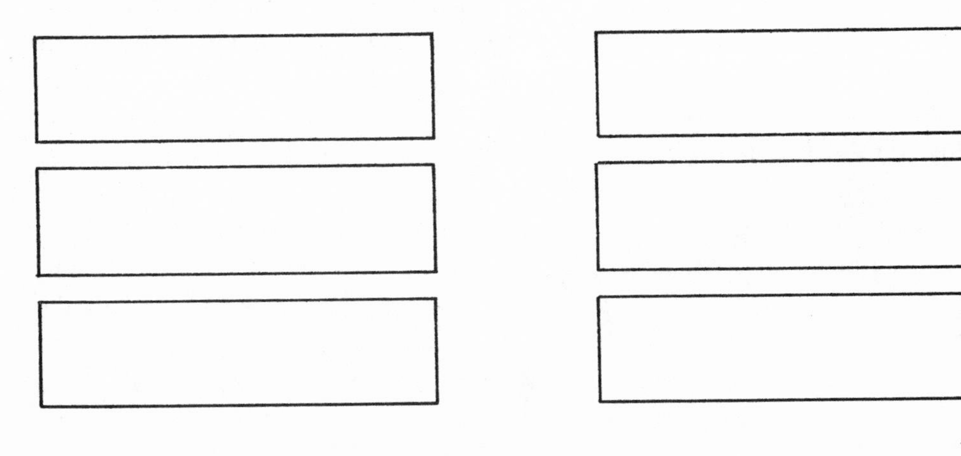

Now, cut one triangle shape from the first strip.

Cut two triangle shapes from the second strip.

Cut three triangle shapes from the third strip.

Cut one square shape from the fourth strip.

Cut two square shapes from the fifth strip.

Cut three square shapes from the sixth strip.

When you are finished you should have six strips with shapes cut out, six triangles, and six squares.

Here's what the strips and cutouts should look like.

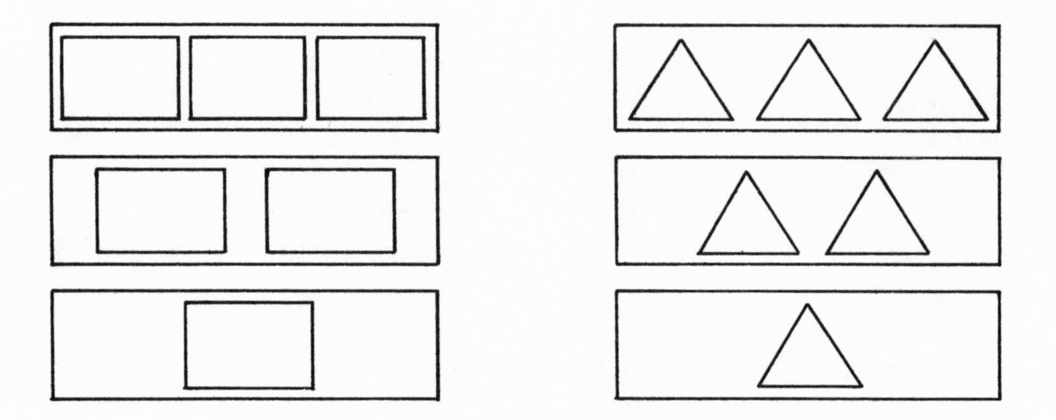

Start out by letting the child examine all the cards and cutouts. You can let him feel the different shapes, too. Gently put his finger around a square opening and then around the triangle. Talk to him about it: "Feel the square? Feel how it goes straight. Here's a corner, and then it goes straight again."

After the child is familiar with all the materials, you can play a matching game together.

Put all the cutouts in a pile between you and the child. Lay out two cards that have different shapes on them. Start out by laying a triangle cutout on the triangle shape. Say, "See, those two have the same shape, don't they? Now it's your turn." Encourage the child to match one of the cutouts with its shape. If he places the cutout correctly, praise him. If he doesn't, continue to match the shapes yourself, and remember to talk to him about what you're doing. If he's not too interested, wait for another time, or try the next game.

Lay all the cards in a pile. Pick out the card with one triangle on it. Show it to the child and ask him, "Which one goes with this card?"

If he chooses a card with another triangle on it, encourage him to sort the rest of the cards by their shapes, all the triangles together and all the squares together.

When he's a little older, he may decide to sort by number. If he picks the card with one square on it, then let him sort the rest of the cards by number: one square with one triangle, two squares with two triangles, three squares with three triangles.

He'll not only be dealing with shapes, but in early ideas of number. There's a big difference between being able to recite "1, 2, 3, 4, . . ."—which he may learn by rote—and really being able to understand the connection between the word "two" and the idea that it follows the number one and means two of something. Children are usually in school before they completely get the connection, but games like this lay the foundation.

PICTURE CARDS

You can make these picture cards by tracing drawings onto cardboard cards about three by five inches. Put the front on one side and the back on the other side of the card. Start out with mother, child, and dog, for instance.

Cards with familiar objects and people on them will give a child a good chance to do a lot of talking. The cards can also be used to teach him new words, new ideas, and new ways to think about these familiar objects.

You can use these picture cards in many ways. Start out by letting the child look at the cards by himself.

Often you can decide the best way to use the cards by watching the way a child plays with them and talks about them.

Whichever way you decide to use the picture cards, remember to talk clearly about what you are doing, and to encourage the child to talk. When the child begins to tell you about what he is doing or seeing, be sure to praise him. For example: "That's right, that's the dog's tail, very good."

Later in the book there will be other ways to use these cards. Here we are interested in their use in sorting and matching.

MATCHING

To use the cards for a matching game will help a child learn to pick out objects which are like, or different from, the familiar objects on the picture cards. Also, like all the other picture-card activities, the matching game will provide a good chance for you and the child to talk together.

Start out by sitting down with the child. Explain that you are going to look through a magazine together. "Come on, Jimmy, let's look at all the pretty pictures in this magazine."

When the child becomes interested in looking through the magazine, ask him if he can "match" one of the picture cards with a picture in the magazine.

"Let's see if we can find a boy in this magazine who looks like the boy on the card."

Go through the magazine together looking for a matching picture.

If the child wants to talk about other things he sees in the magazine, encourage him. Any talking is great, so remember to reward it.

BUILDING AN UNDERSTANDING OF PATTERNS

One of our basic needs is for order. When we get up in the morning we need to know we can count on certain things happening. In the first section, we showed the child games which taught him about grouping, a basic way in which we arrange or order life. Here we are going to show him another way to arrange or order: by patterns. Our purpose is to help the child learn to arrange objects (either by grouping or placing them in order) by shape, size, or color.

The child learns a pattern by recognizing when objects are the same and when they are different. He has to learn to go from the pattern he sees —a red bead, a blue bead, a red bead—to guessing that the next bead will be blue. Since beads come in different shapes, he can find a pattern in shape as well as color. In this first game, our aim is not to have him guess a pattern, but just to learn to copy and see patterns. This gives him a base for "guessing" when he's a little older.

Each of these games is "stretchable." As you come to know what your child can do, you can move the game along to the harder parts, such as more complicated patterns, or guessing what comes next. Let your child set the pace; he'll show when he's ready for tougher ideas, when he wishes to stay where he is for a while, and when he wants to even go back to an easier activity that he can do rapidly.

STRING OF BEADS

Get a shoe string, or a piece of twine, and beads of various shapes and colors. Each bead should have a hole running lengthwise through the middle, and be from one-half to one inch long.

The two- to three-year-old child has trouble using his fingers with any skill. Stringing beads can help to develop his manual skill and his perception. Beads can be used in many matching games and in imaginative play. For instance, they can serve as cargo for trucks and as toy food. But for now we'll talk about their use in teaching patterns.

Very little direction is necessary to get children to string beads. If at first they don't know what to do with the beads, they'll find out very quickly. Let them play with the beads for a while and see if they can discover how to string for themselves. If they can't, it's an easy job to teach them. The best way to start is to make it a cooperative effort. Have the child hold the string. Say, "Watch this! I'm going to take this big red bead and put it on this string. Here it goes . . . whee . . . right down to the bottom. Do you want to try that? O.K., put the string between your thumb—this is your thumb—and this finger [index finger]. Now put the bead on the string. There it goes. Good!" Some children may have trouble holding the string with their fingers and getting the bead on the end of the string. A few demonstrations and they'll be able to do it themselves. After a child has strung an entire string of beads, tie the ends of the string in a knot and make a necklace for him to wear. Some children enjoy wearing necklaces and some do not. For those that do, it's a good incentive to learn to string the beads.

After the child has learned to string the beads, you can move him into stringing only a particular color or shape, and then into stringing patterns. Some children will do this without your help, but others will need it. One method is to try to get the child into a matching game. Say, "I'm going to put on a blue bead. Can you find a blue bead and put it on the string? You *did* find a blue one! Now I'm going to put on another blue bead. Can you find another blue bead?" He may not know "blue", so you can say, "one that is the same color as mine." In this way you are teaching the child to observe as well as providing the exercise needed for eventual skill in writing, drawing, and other manual activities.

Another variation of this game requires two strings—one for the child and one for you. Let the child take the lead. When he strings a bead, say, "Oh, you put on a green bead. I'm going to put on a green bead, too." Then, "Now you've put on a blue bead. I'm going to put one on, too. Look, my string and your string are just alike. You have a green bead and a blue bead, and I have a green bead and a blue bead. Our strings are alike." Once in a while make a mistake to keep the game lively and fun. After a while you can change roles; you lead on your string and let him match on his. The chance to teach the child more language comes about as a natural part of play with the beads. "Same," "different," "on," "off," "into," and "out of" are all words that can be used easily and naturally with the string of beads. As you emphasize these words, the concepts they represent and the words themselves are learned by the child.

This is a toy that children enjoy manipulating on their own. Remember to leave the child time of his own to do his own thing. Let him play at whatever he wants to play. This is one of the toys that he will choose.

BUILDING DISCS

To play this next set of games you will need some discs cut from a wooden dowel about the circumference of a bottlecap, and a poster board cut into five-by-one-inch rectangles. Paint or color some of the discs.

Sit on the floor with the child. Put all the materials in front of the two of you. As you play with the materials talk about them with the child. For example, start putting the discs one on top of the other and say, "Look," I'm stacking these up. I wonder how high we can stack them." Watch to see what he does and talk to him about it: "You're building them up" or "You made them fall down." *Accept everything he does that is constructive, such as stacking, examining, making a row.* Keep talking about what he is doing and what you are doing. "I'm making a bridge. I'll roll a disc under the bridge. Now you try rolling one under."

Let him play with the materials until he has built a couple of things. Then try making some of the patterns shown below. Divide up the discs and rectangles, one for the child and one for yourself, until you have enough to play with. Say, "let's make one just like this one." Point to the pattern you have chosen. "I'll put out a disc here." Help him do all of the first pattern by placing one disc or rectangle at a time on the pattern and waiting for him to put the same disc or rectangle in his pattern. Keep talking as you work.

If the child enjoys making the patterns, let him play teacher for a while. Say, "Now it's your turn to show me some patterns. It's your turn to show me what to do." Copy whatever he makes.

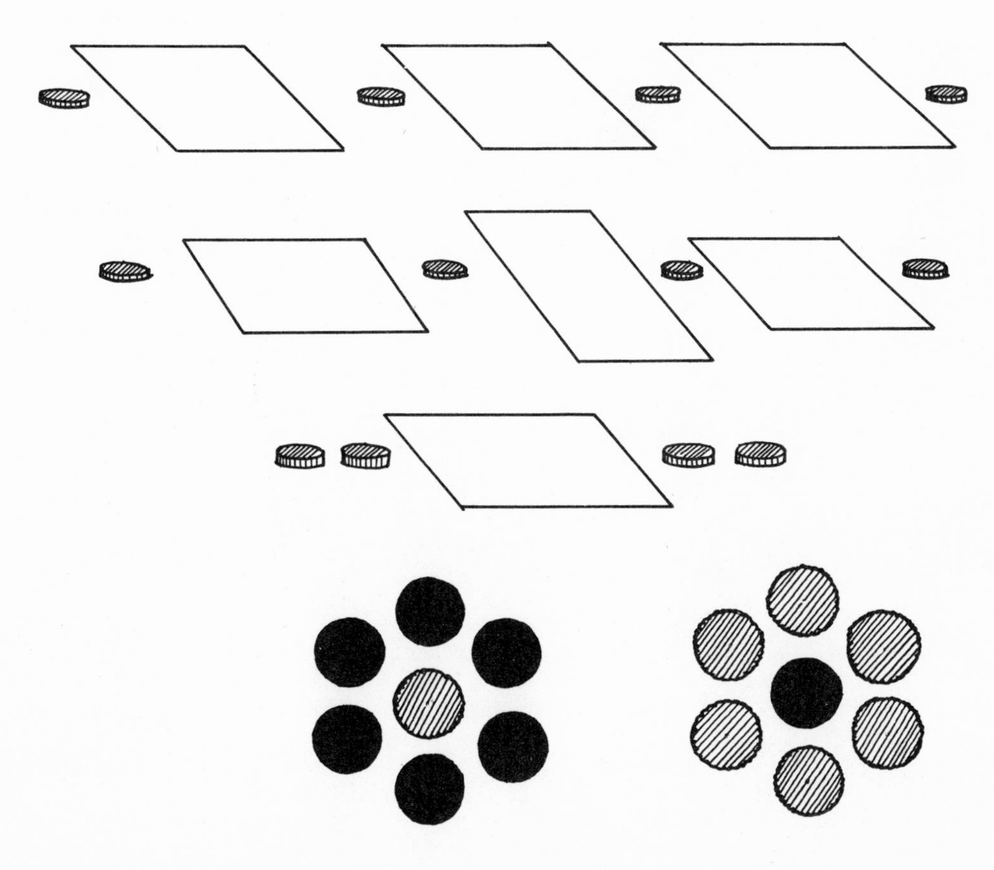

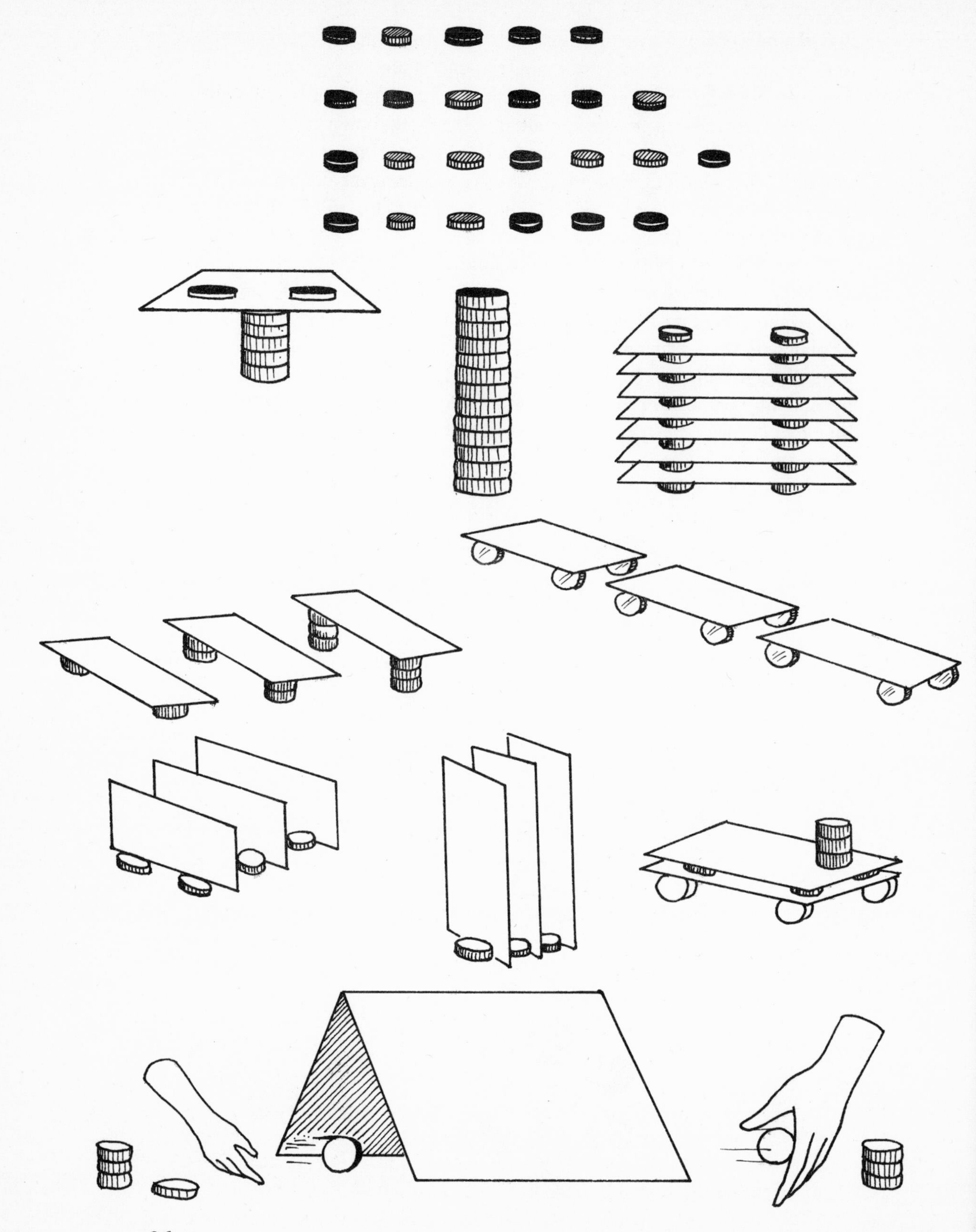

STORY STRIPS

In order for a child to learn to read, he must have certain skills. One of these is the ability to follow a story in order from left to right, beginning to end. You can use the story strips here to help a child learn this.

The story strips can also help a child to think in a logical way. Each picture is a little different from the one preceding it. For example, in the first picture the feet are bare; in the next picture one sock is on. As you work with him on these story strips, he will begin to see things happening one after the other.

You can make your own story strips for the child if you wish. They should present a simple story in a logical order.

Encourage him to look at all the story strips. Then ask him to pick out one to work on. "Which one would you like to talk about? O.K., let's look at this one about shoes."

Try to get the child to talk to you about what he sees. You can ask him, "What is happening here?" or "What do you think will happen next?"

If the child doesn't want to tell you about the story, then you can begin to describe it to him. Talk slowly. If he wants to interrupt and start talking himself, great! Having *him* talk is what you're trying to accomplish!

First, look at each picture separately and talk about it with the child. Always point out the order of the story. For example:

Picture #1 "See, the feet are bare. They don't have any shoes or socks on them."
Picture #2 "Now look. One sock is on."
Picture #3 "Let's see what happens next. Now there are two socks on the feet."
Picture #4 "Oh look, now he's got one shoe on."
Picture #5 "Here comes the other shoe. Now both feet have socks and shoes on."
Picture #6 "One shoe is tied now."
Picture #7 "Now the other shoe is tied, too."
Picture #8 "O.K., the feet have *socks* and *shoes* on, all tied and finished."

Then, if the child is still interested, you can reverse the order. Start with the last picture and work back to the first one.

After you and he have finished the first story, you can continue with the other story strips in the same way. Remember to take your lead from the child. See how he wants to do it. Then you can be sure of his interest.

When he is a little older, you might try scrambling the order by cutting the strip into separate scenes. Have him put them in order and tell you why it goes that way. The idea that events go in some order is a basic one for his understanding of most school subjects and also his own daily life.

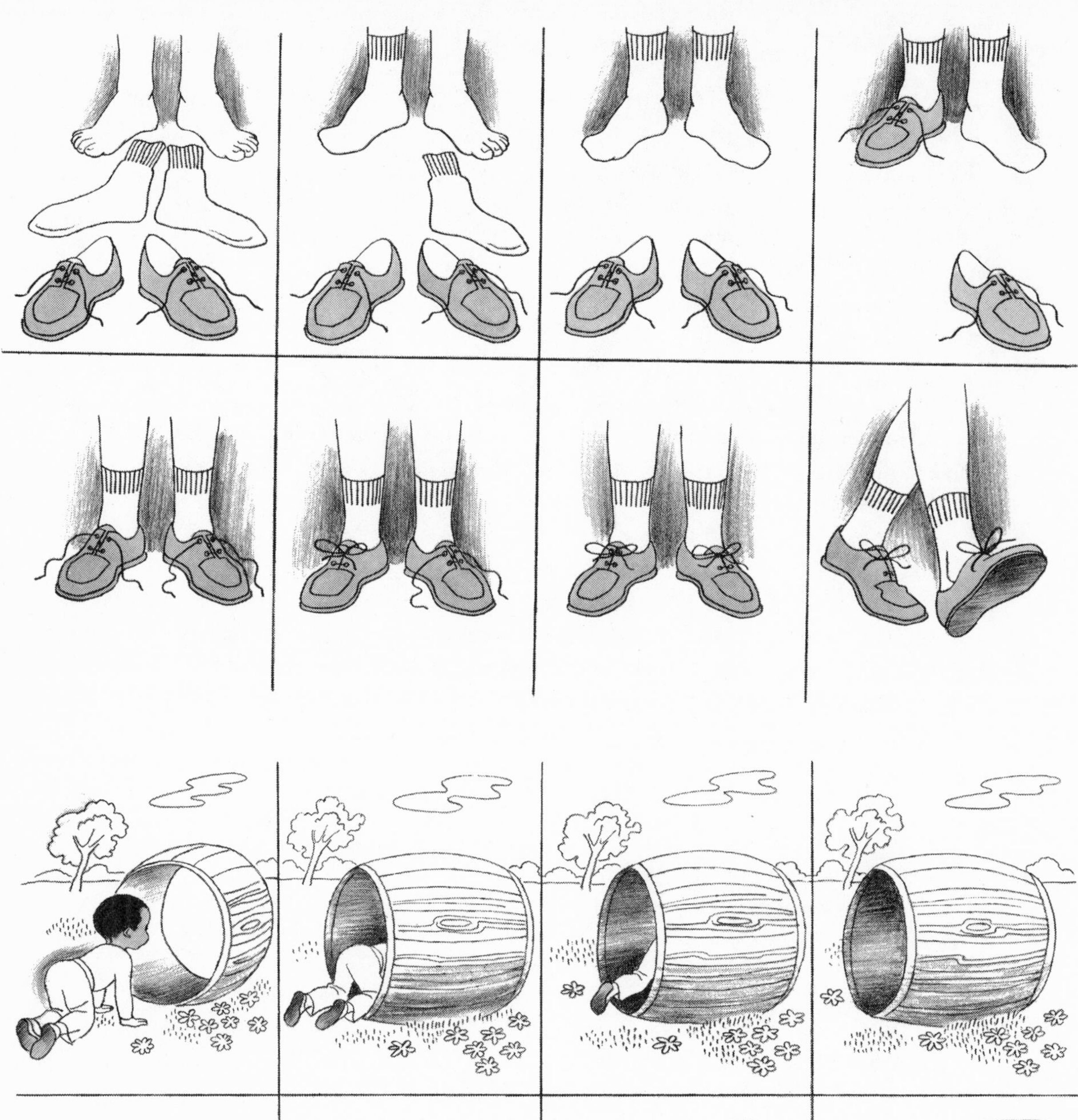

NUMBER PATTERNS

You'll need six sticks or toothpicks for yourself and six for the child. Make the pattern while he watches. "Here's one stick. Here are two sticks. And here are three sticks." Let the child try copying what you've made right underneath your pattern. Talk about what he needs to do. "First you put one stick. Now you put two sticks. Now you put three sticks." As we mentioned before, there is a difference between reciting numbers and using them. Children learn number ideas from handling real objects. This game is an introduction to the idea that a group of objects goes together with a number. Before now, he has piled and sorted. Here all the objects are the same: the only clue is number.

COLOR PATTERNS

Have the child help you color some popsicle sticks. Crayons are fine. Then lay out a color pattern and show your child how to copy it. For example: "I put red, yellow, and another red—two red sticks and a yellow stick—in the middle." Let the child make a pattern for you to copy. The focus here is on color, but you can also talk about the number of sticks.

"GUESS WHICH HAND"

An old and simple game with children is to hide an object in one hand, make two fists, and ask the child to guess which hand the object is in. You can make it a learning game by having a pattern in mind—you can always place the object in your right hand. After your child has guessed correctly several times, ask him if he can tell you why. He may not be able to put in into words. Tell him, "I'm going to hide it differently now (don't say, "In my other hand!") and see if he looks in your left hand. When he gets it right each time, say, "I'm going to do it differently now," and hide it again in your right hand.

You can also make this harder by setting up a pattern—two rights and then a left, for example—and see how fast he learns to figure it out.

EGG CARTONS

Egg cartons made of styrofoam, (a plasticlike cardboard), are an excellent toy for children.

Let the child examine the egg carton. Let him open and close it until he knows how it works. Then say, "Let's play a game. Watch what I do." Put one marble in each of the twelve pockets. If the child wants to put some in, too—encourage him! Then tell him, "Now we're going to hide the marbles with cotton balls." Put a cotton ball over each marble. Again encourage him to do it himself. You can work on this together, taking turns. You can talk about how hard the marble is and how soft the cotton is. With the introduction of other articles of similar texture the child can learn the concepts of hardness and softness.

You can use an egg carton to place the marbles and cotton in a pattern. Encourage the child to help you complete the pattern. You can use these patterns in much the same way a puzzle is used. First, make a pattern and see if the child can make one like it.

Pattern #2 1 marble, 1 cotton ball
1 marble, 1 cotton ball
Pattern #1 2 marbles, 2 cotton balls
2 marbles, 2 cotton balls

Do this until all the pockets are filled.

MUSIC BOXES

There are several types of patterns that children need to learn as they grow. Earlier, we stressed patterns of objects—by shape, by color, by number, by use, and by order. Beginning in infancy, your child started to grasp another kind of pattern—the pattern of the connection between two events, such as a parent entering his vision and his then being picked up, fed or changed. In that situation, his parent controls what happens. He has perhaps had some early experience in manipulating objects such as a cradle toy, which gave him a chance to control a little part of his world.

Now you can make this second type of pattern-learning more visible to the child. One way to do this is with a toy such as a music box. For example, you can say, "Do you know what will happen if I turn this little knob? Watch and listen." Turn the knob a few times so that several notes are played, then say, "Did you hear that? The music played after I turned the knob." Show him how to wind it himself. Don't insist that the child tell you that if he turns the knob then the music will play. Help him see that when it winds down, the music stops and that the playing is due to the winding.

Music boxes hold a fascination for children that exceeds that of adults. They like to play with them for long periods of time. So let them! Music boxes are enjoyed by two- to three-year-olds because of the noise they make. If the music played is familiar and simple, (like "Mary Had a Little Lamb" or "Twinkle, Twinkle Little Star,") then the children can learn the song and sing along with the music box.

There are a variety of other activities to make cause-and-effect clearer to the child, even though he can't understand *why* it happens—such as light and TV switches and all the other gadgets in the home.

RECOGNITION GAMES

The three main goals of this section are to give the child practice in guessing (inference-making), seeing the connection between parts and wholes, and exploring what can't easily be seen. The child will use these skills in many ways as he grows. For example, recognizing an object from one of its known parts is a concept that is part of learning to read. He will not only figure out how to pronounce a word but also guess its meaning from the rest of the sentence. Sometimes we guess how people will act from bits of information we have about them. Guessing and testing that guess is also a basic tool of the scientist. The following activities are geared toward helping the child develop his guessing ability.

TASTING, TESTING

This is a good mealtime activity in the home. The child learns that he can tell what something is by knowing only one fact about it: in this case, taste. Just as we learn what red is by looking at it, we learn what sweet is by tasting something sweet. To distinguish between tastes, compare two things that taste entirely different; for example, salt and sugar. Their appearance is similar, but they do not taste alike.

Let the child taste the salt. Say, "How does that taste? That tastes salty!"

Next, give him some sugar. Ask, "How does that taste? Is it the same? No, it tastes sweet. Now I'm going to hide them behind my back. Now can you tell me which is salt and which is sugar?"

Let the child taste the salt or sugar and tell you how it tastes. If the child is not able to distinguish between the two, say, "I think this is sugar. You taste it again and see what you think."

After this, either at home or in a center, you can extend the game by asking, "How else would you know it's chocolate [or lemon, or strawberry]?" Use those cases where color, shape, or texture are good clues. Salt and pepper, mustard and ketchup, are good examples. By this approach, your child will begin to see that an object can be described by sight, sound, feel, and taste—many senses rather than one. This idea later helps him to group by more than one fact in math, science, and even social studies. He learns to look for several facts before he settles for an easy answer.

"NOW HEAR THIS"

So far in this section we have had games using language, sight, taste, and motor approaches to guessing and recognizing familiar objects. You can also use sound and touch.

One way to play with an egg carton is to let the child put marbles in the carton, close the cover, and shake it. Say, "Listen to those noisy marbles." Then put in cotton balls after you have taken out the marbles, close the cover, and shake the carton. Ask, "What's inside now?" or "See, the cotton doesn't make noise like the marbles."

You can, of course, substitute cans, boxes, paper bags for the cartons, and anything that can shake and rattle for marbles. This is not an easy game, because many things sound alike. Start with objects that sound different enough so that your child can win the game.

BLIND MAN'S BLUFF

Touch is also a very valuable way for the child to explore his world. He has been touching things since birth, and he has used his hands to find out many things. Naturally, he has seen what he is touching, so that these two senses have worked together as pathways for learning.

It's a lot harder to recognize objects by touch alone. It makes a child notice facts, such as the hardness or heaviness of something, that he can't find out just by looking.

Take some familiar objects and put them in a box (or bag, or can) and have the child close his eyes. (Blindfolds may be frightening—it's better, even if he peeks, to let *him* control his sight.) Ask him to pull out an object that is hard, soft, or thin. Then vary the game by asking for objects by name: a marble, a stick, a crayon. A third variation is to ask for an object that can roll, one with which you can wipe, one with which you can write, one that's a toy. A fourth variation is to ask for a piece of paper, a piece of wood, a piece of cloth, a piece of cotton, a piece of metal, etc.

What has the child learned besides the fact he can tell what things are by touching them? He's learned that the same object can be pulled out of the box for more than one reason. For instance, a marble is hard, can roll, is made of glass, and is a toy. These properties of the marble tie in this game with the sorting and pattern games in the first two sections. Any game can serve a number of purposes if you use it that way.

A word of caution: Don't try all these variations at once. Stretch them over a month or so, so that you come back to a familiar game but give it a new twist.

FILLING IN THE LINES

Here is another way to help your child see that he can build a finished idea (in this case, a face) when he is shown a part. In this game of completing a drawing, it is best to give him a "broken" line rather than a blank space. It is another form of "guess what."

Let the child look at the two faces on the next page. Point out how the two faces are alike. Ask, "Is this face [point to one] the same as the other face? Are both their eyes looking in the same direction?"

Then turn the page. Let the child look at the faces. Help him notice that the lower face has a line that needs to be drawn in. Say, "Look, part of the face isn't finished here [point to the broken line]. Let's draw it in so it will be the same as the other face."

The adult can draw one picture in if the child does not understand. The adult should turn to the next page and again point out the missing part of the face. The complete face is always above and the incomplete one below. Each page has more of the incomplete face missing. The adult should guide the child's hand if he still doesn't understand.

You can design your own sheets, using houses, chairs, cars, or any other objects. Remember, we are counting on you to use your creativity to build your own games or variations from these!

Children sometimes are more interested in telling stories about the pictures than in completing the pictures. If this is the case, by all means let them. Maybe later the child will understand and want to finish the pictures.

STRIP TEASE I

The purpose of this game is to develop your child's skills in recognizing a whole when he sees just a part of it. As we said in the introduction to this section, this is a basic and useful skill in problem-solving, especially in science.

Cut several large, colorful pictures from a magazine. For example, a ball, a baby, a car, a TV set, or a shoe would be good. Make a covering sheet for the pictures out of any ordinary eight-and-a-half-inch by ten-inch piece of paper. Cut the top sheet in strips from right to left, leaving about one inch of uncut paper on the left (see illustration).

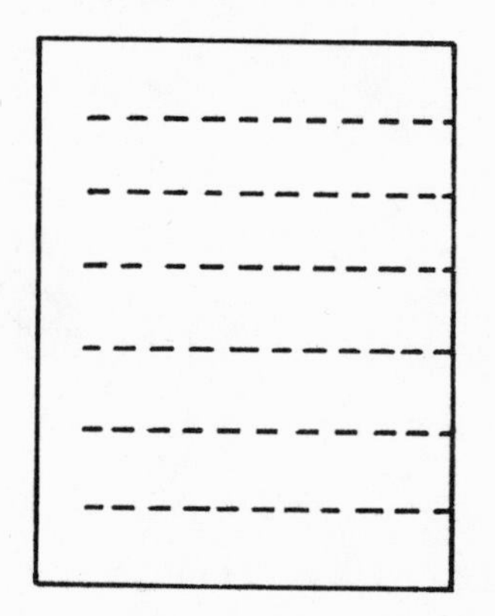

First, show each picture to the child and make sure he knows the name of the object in the picture. For example, say, "Here's a picture of a ball. You have a ball, don't you? Does this look like your ball?"

After you are sure that the child knows the name of the object in each picture say, "Now we are going to play a game. I'm going to cover up each picture. Then I'm going to uncover just a little bit of it and see if you can tell me what it is." Then take a picture and cover it up with the covering sheet. Pull back one strip and say, "You can see a little bit of this picture.

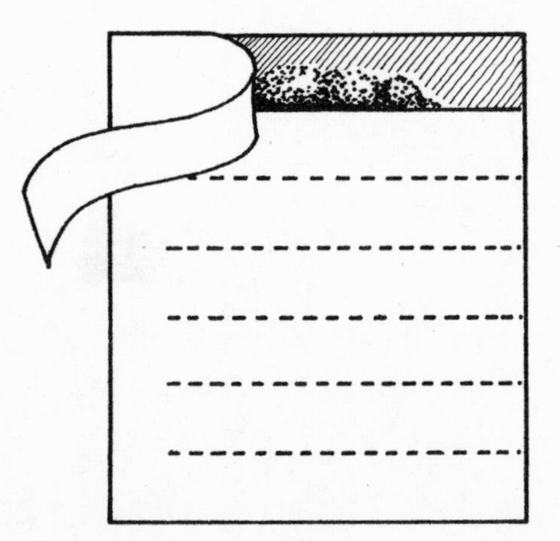

Can you guess what it is?" If the child guesses right away, say something like, "How did you guess that so fast? I didn't know what it was." Or if he doesn't, say, "O.K., here's another piece. Boy, this is hard. I wonder what this is?"

Keep talking about each picture, uncovering it a little bit at a time, until the child finally guesses what it is. When he does guess correctly, be sure to praise him.

Remember this is a game for having fun. If the child gets tired of doing it, stop for a while and come back to it later.

WHICH ONE?

Here is another game which uses the picture cards. This game will help a child learn new words and teach him to follow directions.

Start out by laying the three picture cards out in front of you and the child.

Now give a hint about one of the cards. For example:

"Which one barks 'Woof!' "

"Which one has a dress?"

"Which one wags his tail?"

Then *you* can start out by picking out a card. "Here's one that barks. He's the dog."

Put the card back and let the child have a turn. "O.K., now it's your turn. Which one wags his tail?"

If he picks the dog, praise him. "Good, that's the dog. He barks and he wags his tail."

If the child picks the wrong card, point out some things about the card he chooses instead of just telling him that he is wrong.

You can probably think of your own hints about the cards. If the child wants to, let him make up his hints and *you* choose from the three cards.

THROUGH THE MAGNIFYING GLASS

Up to now, although we've used different senses—sight, sound, touch, taste—all the objects have been familiar, and the facts about them easy to see (or touch, taste, or hear)! Your child may now enjoy a new type of discovery: that there are many facts about a familiar object he *can't* easily see. For him, at this time, he may get the pure fun of discovery out of this. But there is a deeper lesson which will only be learned over a period of time, even though it starts here. It is that there are facts of nature that exist even if we can't see or explain them.

For this activity you will need a small magnifying glass and several different things to look at. A bottlecap, a penny, a piece of cotton, a newspaper, some cloth, a popsicle stick, a flower, and a leaf are just a few of the things you can easily find which will be fun to look at through the magnifying glass.

First, show your child how to hold the glass an inch or two away from what he's looking at, so he can see it clearly. Then encourage him to look at several objects through the glass, pointing out how much bigger they look. "See how much bigger the penny looks when we use the magnifying glass?"

Have the child look at just part of an object, like a popsicle stick, so he can easily see the difference the magnifying glass makes. By moving the glass slowly from one end of the stick to the other the child can see the stick get larger as the glass passes over it. "Look how much smaller the ends of the stick seem than the middle, where the glass is!"

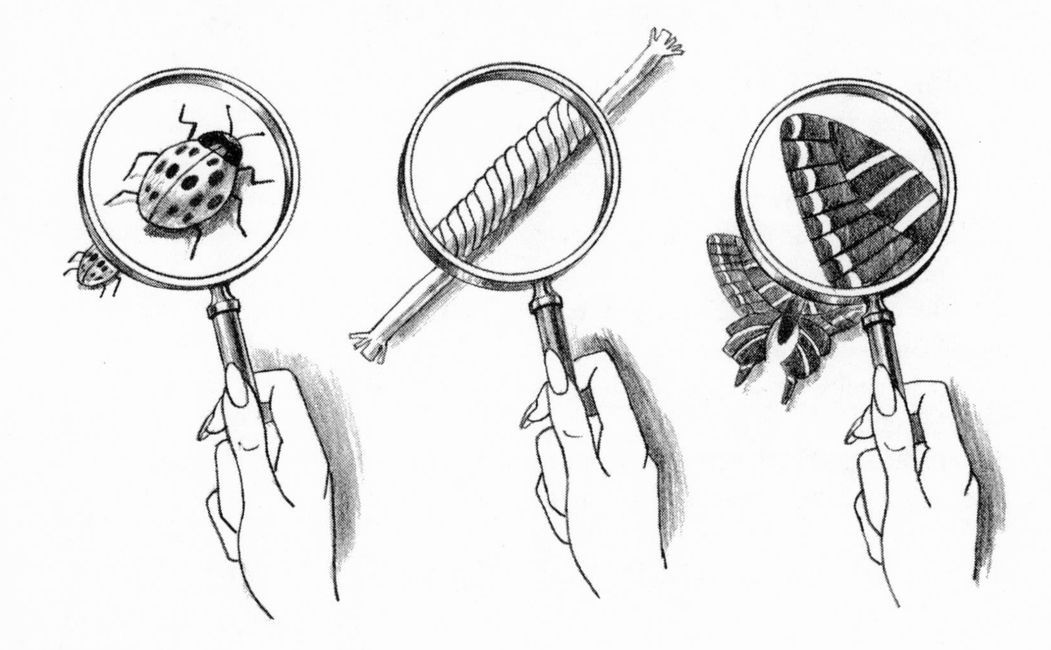

Try to find things that actually look different—not just bigger—under the magnifying glass. A picture from the newspaper, a piece of cotton, or some grains of sand are appropriate objects. Describe what you see when looking through the glass and compare that with what you see without it. For example, with the newspaper picture, you can say, "See all the little dots? The picture is really made up of lots and lots of little dots. But we can't see the dots without the magnifying glass."

Animate objects—ants, worms, and the like—are also fascinating under the magnifying glass.

The child will probably find many interesting things to look at on his own. Encourage him to explore with his new toy. Realizing that some things are too small to see without a special glass and that you can see some things better if you make them bigger, are two more steps in your child's ever-broadening knowledge of the world.

WORD PLAY

The years from two to four are one of the most important times for language and speech development. The child learns not only vocabulary, but also language rules—such as the arrangement of words in sentences—from hearing you. This ability to understand what you're saying is the basis for his learning to talk.

In this section, the games are geared toward the use of words. We also develop in the child's mind the idea that words are not only heard and spoken, but also written down. Some of these activities are beginning experiences for later reading. But they are *not* the same as the teaching of reading. Our aim in this section is to help the child learn more about words that are not just labels (such as "dog," "man") but that deal with location in space ("on," "near," "far"). This ties in with the learning games in the first section in which the child worked with objects that taught him about space, such as the problem-solving toys.

In playing these games, remember this general rule: If your child is interested, you're on the right track. If he's bored, let him go on to some other activity. This is especially important in word play, because it is very easy to slide into drill and rote recitation.

SELF TALK

Talking with a child about things, people, and ideas is one of the most important ways he learns. Sometimes adults forget to take advantage of this chance to talk with children. Remember, talking with a child is teaching a child, even if he doesn't, or can't, talk back.

Here are some ways to use everyday activities to talk about and to help the child learn words and ideas.

Talk to the child out loud about all the things *you* are doing and seeing. Let the child know there are words for all kinds of activities and things. If you try to talk slowly and clearly it will help the child get more out of what you say. Here's an example of an everyday thing that you do and how it can be used as an opportunity to talk to a child: As you clean up a room talk clearly about everything you do. Make sure the child is paying attention. As you talk he will become more interested in you and your words.

"See, I'm putting the block in the bag."

"Here's a red block going in. Now I'll get a blue one."

"Now I'll put the bag on the shelf."

If the child wants to help you with your activity, fine. Then you can talk about his actions.

"Look, Jimmy is putting all the marbles in the box."

"You're picking up the books now."

Talking about your activities and the child's activities will be interesting to him. Pretty soon he might start talking back to you!

"WHAT'S YOUR NAME?"

A child should learn his name early. A child's name is his identity. Knowing his name makes a child feel important. It helps him realize that he is a separate and important person in a world filled with many things.

There are many ways to use and emphasize one name. First, remember that a child should *always* be called by his name. He will learn his name and be proud of it only if you use it a lot. Use his nickname, too. Remember, a child can't learn who he is and that he counts, if he doesn't learn his own special name that belongs to him.

Throughout the day, try to remember to say his name whenever you talk to him. For example, "Jimmy, please give me those blocks."

One way to see if a child can tell you his name is by using a mirror. Let him see his face in a mirror and say, "Who is that?" If he doesn't answer,

say to him, "See, that's you. That's *Jimmy*." Make sure that he is looking at his image while you talk about it. Then try again. Make a game out of it. Show the child his image and say, "Who is that boy [girl]?" Encourage *him* to say his own name.

Another way to try to emphasize his name is to play a game of hide and seek.

You'll need a towel or large cloth for this. Use it to hide the child's face by placing the cloth in front of it.

Now say, "Where did *Jimmy* go?" "I can't see Jimmy." "Where is *Jimmy* hiding?" When the child removes the towel and shows you his face, say, "There's *Jimmy*. I see *Jimmy*."

Soon Jimmy can begin to answer himself by saying his name: "Here is Jimmy."

FINGER PLAY RHYMES

There are many songs and rhymes for children which can be used as the basis for hand-and-finger games. These games give a child the chance to exercise his smaller muscles. They also help him learn that words can be fun. These games can be played with an individual child and with a group of children. You'll be surprised at how much fun you and the children can have with them. Give them a try! Here are the lyrics to some common ones:

ROW, ROW, ROW YOUR BOAT

Row, row, row your boat
Gently down the stream.
Merrily, merrily, merrily, merrily,
Life is but a dream.

JACK-IN-THE-BOX

Jack-in-the-box
Sits so still.
Won't you come out?
Yes! I will!

HANDS

Open, shut them, open, shut them.
Give a little clap.
Open, shut them, open, shut them.
Put them in your lap.

Creeping, creeping, creeping, creeping,
Right up to your chin,
Open wide your little mouth, BUT
Do not put them in!

TEENSY, WEENSY SPIDER

A teensy, weensy spider
Climbed up the water spout.
Down came the rain
And washed the spider out.

Out came the sun
And dried up all the rain
And the teensy, weensy spider
Climbed up the spout again.

PEASE PORRIDGE HOT

Pease porridge hot.
Pease porridge cold.
Pease porridge in the pot
Nine days old.

Some like it hot.
Some like it cold.
Some like it in the pot
Nine days old.

PICTURE CARDS

The picture cards described in the first section can be used to teach new words and ideas to the child and help him learn to follow directions.

First, let the child look at the cards. Make sure he sees the back of each card. You can point this out to him—"You saw the front of the dog, now look, here is his back."

Then you can help the child understand some new words by giving him simple directions to follow and talking about what you do.

"Let's put the mommy to bed now."

"I'll put the dog to bed; you lay the mommy down so she can go to sleep."

If the child places the figure on the card on its back, talk about that: "The mommy is going to sleep on her back." Then you can place the dog card on its front and talk about that.

"I'll put the dog to bed on his front side. The mommy can sleep on her back and the dog sleeps on his front."

Let the child take the lead and place his card the way he likes. Then you can talk about and use your card to teach him a different word. You can do this for front and back.

You can talk about the front and back of both of you, too. This will help him get the idea.

"Here's your front, Jimmy. See where the buttons on your shirt go."

"I'll turn around and show you my back. It's like the mommy's back on the card." (Point out the back of the card.)

There are many other new words and ideas which you can teach a child with these cards. Some of these are *near, far, next to, on top of, between,* and *upside down.* You can probably think of others.

These words are commonly used by adults, but they often are confusing to young children. If you use picture cards to teach a child about these words, it will help him understand and speak better.

Here's an example of how to use the picture cards to help a child learn some of these new words:

Lay two of the cards out next to each other. Let the child hold the third card.

Start out by making a pile out of your cards and his card. Say to the

child, "Look, I'll put one on top. Now you take yours and put it *on top* of mine."

If he is able to do it, praise him. If he doesn't seem to understand, show him. Put his card on top of yours. Explain to him what you are doing. Now place your other card on top of both cards. Again, talk about what you're doing. "There now, mine is *on the top,* and look, there is your card right *between* the other two."

You can use the same kinds of games to introduce some of the other new words. For example, if you want to work on *near* and *far,* start out by laying the card with the dog on it down. Let the child hold one card, the boy, and you hold the other, the mother. Place your card far away from the dog.

"Look, I put the mother *far* away from the dog."

Then ask him, "Where do you want to put your card?" Let him place it wherever he wants. If he puts it near the dog, you can talk about this. "You put the boy right *near* the dog. The boy and the dog are near each other but the mother is *far* away."

If he places his card far from the dog, talk about that: "You put the boy *far* from the dog. Now the mother and the boy are *both* far from the dog."

Now you can place your card near the dog. "See how the mother is *near* the dog."

Again ask him to place his card where he wants to. Point out where he has put it: "near" or "far."

STRIP TEASE II

A good game to play to help your child understand that printed words stand for something is to take a product which is known to the child (a cereal box, for example) and cover the front with strips. Lift up the strip that shows the picture of what's inside, and ask him, "What's in the box?" After he tells you, cover that part and lift off the strip with just the name. Ask him, "Now what's in the box? How do you know? Let's look inside!"

Take another product with which he's familiar and cover all but the name. See if he can guess what it is. He may use other clues—such as shape, color, or size—but that's O.K. After he guesses, let him check it out.

You'll be surprised how many names he knows, and he'll get the idea that those funny shapes (letters) tell him something.

BOOKS

Books for two-to-three-year-olds should have more pictures than words. Books with large, clear pictures are best. Pictures of farm animals, zoo animals, and people lend themselves to storytelling and seem to hold children's interest.

If you can't find suitable books, draw your own or get a friend who has some artistic ability to help you.

The mistake most often made by adults showing books to two- and three-year-olds is the adult's insistence on reading the text word for word to the child. Take one page at a time. Imagine that there are no words on the page. Take the child in your lap and look at the first picture. Rather than read what is written on the page, look at the picture and talk to the child about it. Suppose that it is a picture of a policeman directing traffic. You could say, "Look at that policeman. Do you know what he is doing?" Be sure to give the child time to respond. "He is directing traffic. He holds up his hand like this to stop cars. Let me see you hold up your hand to stop the cars. That's good. I see a whistle in his hand. Do you see it? How does a whistle go?"

By talking about each picture and giving the child a chance to talk, too, you can make books very enjoyable for him.

Books are a great means of encouraging language development. But simply reading the words to the child leaves him in the dark about the meaning of the words and how the words and pictures go together. Try describing a picture or pointing to it and having the child describe it.

Gradually, you can point to a picture, then to the word for the picture. You can say, "Here's a picture of a . . . [stop and let your child give you the word, such as 'car']." Then say, "And here's the word 'car.' The word means car." Associating the words and pictures is more important than drilling the child on recognition of words and letters. For the moment, don't try to get the child to memorize words and letters.

Children of this age won't sit still for long while you read to them and turn the pages in an orderly way. Soon they will be turning the pages before you have finished, and the whole activity becomes very frustrating. Read to the child only as long as he is willing to sit still and listen. When he becomes restless, turn the book over to him and leave him with it. Let him play with it alone as much as he wants. He will probably turn the pages over and over looking at the pictures. He may turn the book upside down or try to tear the pages. This is normal for young children. You can encourage him to treat the books with care by setting a good example yourself.

Try to use the books once a day. Make sure that the books are in a place where the child can find them easily.

Spend a lot of time reading with the child. If you're enthusiastic, he will be, too. Make books exciting and fun. The child's early experience with books can carry him through to his school days and lend support to his first attempts to learn how to read.

WRITE YOUR OWN BOOK

A child's special book is a great talk-starter. A child likes to talk about those people and things that are familiar to him. His own book can also lead to an interest in books in general, and can help him understand that books tell about things through pictures and words.

You can make a special book for the child, one that's just for him and that he can keep. By making the book just for the child you'll create a special interest in the book for him. If the book is about *him,* what *he* does and the people *he* knows, he'll be sure to like it and want to look at it with you.

Here is a sample that was used at a pre-school center, it may fit your child, too. If it doesn't, it's easy enough to make your own book, using your own drawings or those you've cut out of magazines and pasted on blank pages. If you make your own book, be sure to leave room at the bottom of each page on which you've drawn or pasted a picture to write a few words about what's happening in the picture.

The way in which you use this book will depend on the child. Some children will sit quietly while a book is read to them. If your child does this, then go through the book starting at the beginning and talking about each picture. Point out all the details as you talk to the child. For example:

#1. "Look, who's that boy? Is that you?"
"There you are all dressed in a shirt, pants, shoes, and socks.
. . . Where are you going?"

Try to get the child involved in the book, but if he just wants to listen, that's fine, too.

Your child may get very excited about the book and want to tell you all about the pictures. If this is the case, encourage him. Then later you can tell him about the pictures or read the book to him.

Remember, *how* you use this book is the most important thing. If you show a child that you are interested and excited about reading this book, he'll be interested, too.

I'm ______________________________.

I go to school today.

I'm ________________________.
I go to school today.

Here is my school.
That's ____________________________, my teacher.

Sometimes I play by myself.

Sometimes I play by myself.

Sometimes I play with others.

My teacher shows me how to cut with scissors.

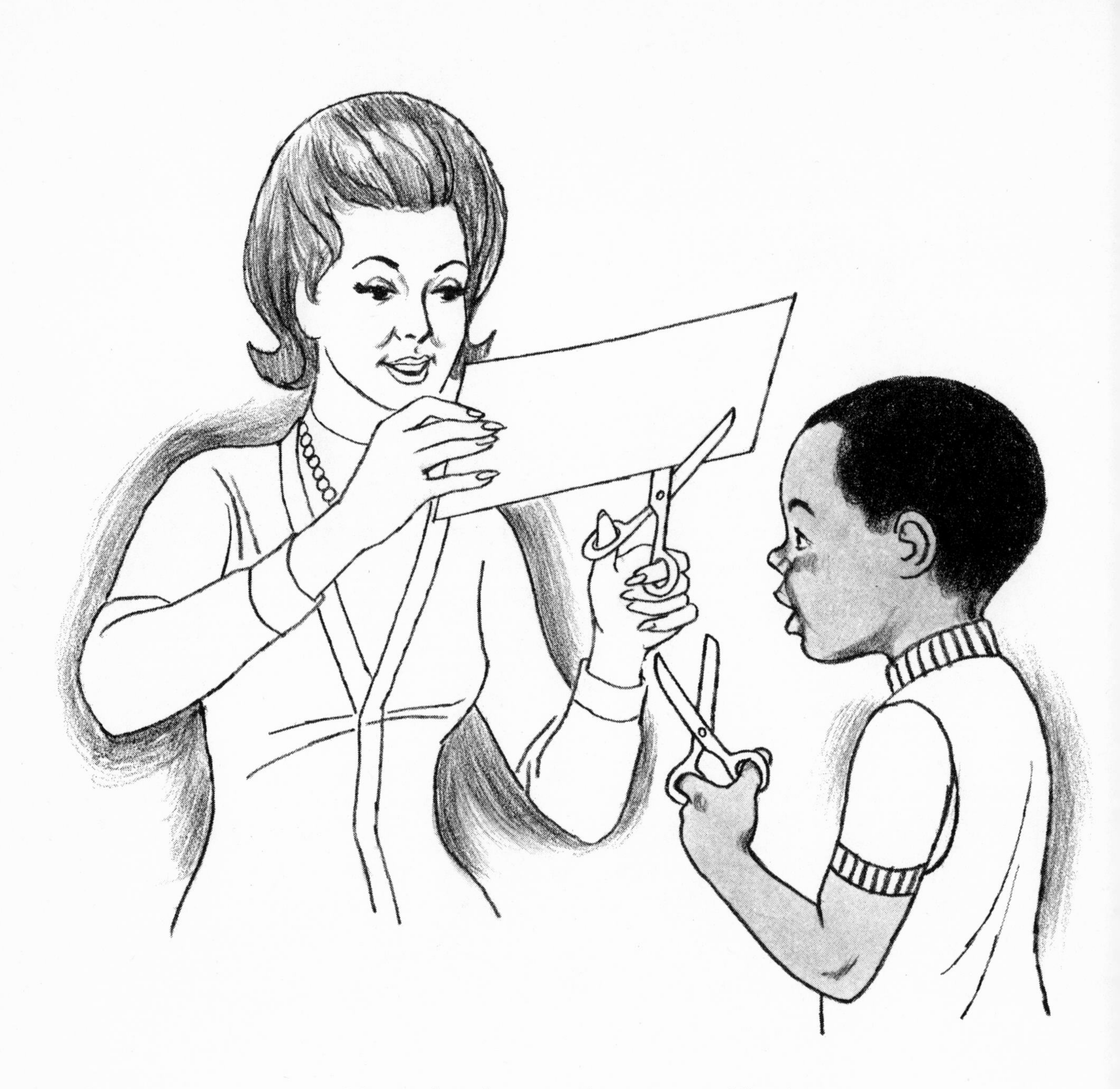

My teacher shows me how to cut with scissors.

Now it's snack time.

I like to draw.

Time to go home.

DEVELOPING PHYSICAL COORDINATION

It is obvious to any parent or caregiver that one thing the young child has (which adults may lack) is energy! The young child is forever active. He needs to run, jump, climb, wrestle, and work off steam. These are also years for improving skill—which is not the same as activity. Here's where you come in: by helping him to use his energy in ways that are fun and that also build skill. The games in this section are designed for that purpose.

There are two sets of muscles which need activity and use, not only for healthy physical development, but also because many reading experts believe that there is a close connection between muscle coordination and reading ability. First, there are the large muscles—in arms and legs—and then the small—in fingers. Skill means getting the muscles to do what we want. To achieve this, the eyes, the brain, and the muscles all have to work together. When the child sees that he can use his body well—he can jump where he wants, get a ball to go where he wants, pick up something small with a tool, hit the nail on the head—he gets a good feeling about himself: a feeling of competence. It is this combination of eye-arm-leg-finger coordination, and the feeling of confidence, that connects these activities with reading, writing, and school work in general.

WALKING THE BEAM

Sometimes children, for one reason or another, don't get exercise in developing their coordination. They don't get practice at doing things which require balancing (making the eyes work with the whole body) and even simple things like walking or crawling. Some authorities believe such skills are related to reading. In any event, they are fun and they give the child a sense of competence. One way to give the child the exercise he needs for balancing, is to play a game that is like walking a tightrope.

Place a two-by-four wooden beam on the floor with the wide side flat. Show the child how to walk on the beam. Probably the easiest way is to place one foot in front of the other foot and walk along. Try this to see if the child can do it. If he can, then try walking the beam by placing one foot directly ahead of the other, heel to toe. Then go on to walking sideways.

After a while try letting him walk backward along the beam. Also, you can play follow the leader with either you or the child leading: jumping off the board, jumping over the board, straddling the board or whatever you can

think of. This can be an exciting game for children, one which they will want to play over and over.

A lot of action words can be learned from this game, too: jump, crawl, over, under, off, walk, backward, and follow.

LET'S PLAY BALL!

We all learn about things, and people, by observing how our actions and behavior affect them. This is one way we also learn how to control our own behavior better. Playing with a ball is a good example of this kind of learning. When a child is able to make the ball do what he wants, he gains general confidence in his ability and in himself.

A child learns about the properties of objects through playing with them. He learns about their similarities, their differences, their weights and their textures. He finds out that some of the motions he used with one ball don't have the same effect on another ball, and that there's an even greater difference in what these same motions make a balloon do.

We can help children learn some of these things a little better and maybe a little sooner by paying more attention to the way we play games. Let's look at some of the ways of playing with a ball.

A good way to start ballplaying is to sit on the floor facing the child, with legs extended, so that your feet touch the child's and form a "playing field." Get a ball that's small enough to leave plenty of room for rolling. Roll it to the child saying, "Here comes the ball. Catch the ball." Be enthusiastic and excited when you talk and play; it's a lot more fun that way. When he gets it, praise him by smiling and saying, "Good catch!" Then continue the game by holding your hands open near the floor and encouraging him to roll the ball back to you:

"All right, Johnny, your turn. Roll the ball to me."

"Good roll, right into my hands."

"My turn now. Ready?"

"Here comes the ball."

If the ball accidentally goes out of the "playing field," make getting it and sitting down again part of the game, too.

Gradually you can move farther apart to give the child an opportunity to increase his skill. If the ball should bounce instead of roll, mention it and make it into a new way to play the game: "The ball bounced that time. You made it bounce. Now I'll bounce the ball back to you. Ready?" If he doesn't catch it the first time you might say, "When the ball bounces it's harder to catch, isn't it?"

"Let's try it again."

"Bounce it back to me."

"Good! You can really bounce the ball."

If it's hard for the child to bounce the ball, stand up and show him how to let go of the ball and watch it bounce up and down on the floor: "See the ball bounce up and down?"

"That's good, you made the ball bounce!"

Then you can show him how to throw the ball at the floor to make it bounce higher. You might even make a game of having him try to catch his bounces before you go back to the bounce-catch game with him.

A young child quickly learns that if he opens his hand, the ball will fall (except if he keeps his palm facing upward). He then learns that by swinging his arm and letting go he can either roll the ball, bounce it, or toss it through the air. Just being able to combine these two simple motions starts a child on his way to playing all sorts of ball games. It's also the beginning of the coordination necessary for other games that require rolling, tossing, or pitching, such as bowling, horseshoes, basketball, and baseball.

Playing games with three or four people gives the child additional practice for improving and expanding his skill, as well as providing the opportunity to begin learning simple rules.

Playing by rules is a part of everyday life. We can help a child begin to understand this by providing examples for him to follow. Examples speak louder than words, so don't spend a lot of time explaining or attempting to enforce rules. Children watch the adults around them for clues on how to behave. Your actions are the rules they're learning.

Here's another rolling game: Lay a wastebasket on its side and try to roll a ball into it. By showing the child the game, you're also showing him the rules:

"Everyone has to stand behind this line; the game is to try to roll the ball into the basket like this [roll the ball yourself]. The person who rolls the ball goes and gets it for the next player [go get the ball]. O.K.? Johnny, here's the ball, you try it."

Start close enough that the child can easily get the ball in. Then move farther away or use an empty coffee can, or even a large glass—anything with a big enough opening for the ball.

This game can be changed into a bouncing game by setting the wastebasket or other container upright and trying to bounce the ball into it. If this game is too hard, go back to a simpler bounce game so the child can practice controlling the bounce of the ball without missing every time.

It's also fun to bounce the ball off the wall. Start by rolling the ball straight at the wall: "See how the ball bounces straight back?" Now try rolling it at an angle and see what happens. You can play a game of catch by rolling the ball into the wall at an angle.

You can also bounce the ball from the floor to the wall and try to catch

it before it hits the floor again. Or the other way around: Toss the ball against the wall and catch it after it bounces off the floor.

As you and the children invent new games, remember all the opportunities for learning that go along with having fun.

BALLS, BALLOONS, AND BUBBLES

Even though we are chiefly working on muscle development, all games offer chances for children to learn new ideas and to practice old skills. Earlier, the child was introduced to recognition games, sorting, and patterns. Here he can extend those skills by seeing how balls, balloons, and bubbles are alike and how they are different. The special twist is that he learns how to change the amount of muscle power he uses to fit the weight and other characteristics of these objects.

Just blowing up a balloon can be an exciting event for a child. Seeing what "makes" a balloon gives the child some hints about how it compares with a ball. Here are just some of the differences a child can see: a ball is the same size all the time, but a balloon gets bigger as we blow more air into it, and smaller if the air gets out; balloons float in the air, balls fall directly to the floor; balloons are more pliable than most balls: "Look, you can push your thumb a long way into the balloon but not into the ball." Balloons also come in many different shapes, but balls are almost always round. If you point out these differences and talk about them, the child learns even faster. Remember, you may have to show the child how to blow up the balloon, or even blow it up for him. As it's being blown up, talk about how the air stretches the balloon and makes it bigger and bigger. Tell the child, "If you blow in too much air, the balloon stretches so thin that it will break."

If the balloon accidentally slips away and races through the air, make this part of the game. Tell the child how the stretched balloon will push the air out much the way he blew it in, if the end is not tied tight.

When the balloons are blown up and the ends securely tied to keep in the air, have the child drop a balloon the way he dropped the ball. "See how the balloon floats down to the floor?" Then drop a ball. "The ball falls straight down to the floor. Balloons aren't as heavy as balls, so they fall slower."

Try some "ball games" with a balloon, rolling or throwing the balloon like you did the ball. The child will have to change his motions to make the balloon go very far: "Try hitting the balloon with your hand instead of throwing it." Soon the child will find he can make the balloon go farther by hitting it instead of throwing it.

Make a game of just trying to keep the balloon in the air by hitting it. You can take turns hitting. "First I'll hit the balloon, then you hit it, then

I'll hit it again, and we'll see how long we can keep the balloon in the air." Tap the balloon gently toward the child so he'll be able to hit it easily.

This game will give the child practice judging distances and controlling his larger muscles, as he tries to hit the balloon before it hits the floor. Remember to talk about the action:

"Wow! That was a high one."

"Oh, I missed! The balloon hit the floor."

"Are you ready? I'm going to hit it—here comes the balloon."

You might be able to keep some balloons up in the air just by blowing on them, but this is easier to do with bubbles. Fill a plastic cup with soap flakes and water and show the child how to blow into the soapy water with a straw: "Look at the bubbles you made."

Make a loop out of fine wire and dip it into the soapy water. Tell the child, "Blow gently, not hard like we did with the balloon," to make larger bubbles. A small amount of cooking oil added to the soapy water should strengthen the bubbles enough so that they will float in the air without breaking.

Show the child how to keep the bubbles floating in the air by blowing gently on them as you did with the balloon.

Breaking the bubbles can be fun, too. "Can you hear it when it breaks? How about breaking balloons? Bang!"

CLOWN PUNCHING BAG

The clown punching bag is made of plastic, is about three feet tall, and blows up like a balloon. It is weighted at the bottom so that it can't be knocked over. The punching bag is best used in a group setting, although it can be used in the home by one child. If you are using it at home, the neighbors' children may want to play. However, check to see if their parents understand and approve of this type of toy, which makes some children get too excited. It's best to supervise the children's use of the bag, to be sure that no one gets hurt or moves from punching the bag to punching another child! This toy can help children learn how to handle their anger, but you will need to watch and place some limits.

All of the games with the clown punching bag promote the strength and confidence of children. Through wrestling, kicking, hitting, and chasing the clown, children develop the muscles used for walking, running, and playing, and they learn to coordinate these muscles. They also learn to play with other children.

Many children are afraid of the punching bag when they first see it and have to be coaxed to play with it. Hold it so that it can't rock back and forth when the child hits it. Hit the clown yourself and say, "Here is a toy that's made for hitting and kicking. Watch this."

Hold on to the punching bag and hit it. Then say to the child, "Now you try it. If the child hits or kicks the clown say, "Good boy!" If he doesn't hit the clown, go through the steps again. Sooner or later the child will want to play with the punching bag, especially if he sees other children doing it.

After the children have become used to the clown, gather several children in a circle. Place the clown in front of one of the children and let him kick it. As one child after another kicks the clown, it will move around the circle. Encourage the children to shout such words as "crack," "wham," "crash," "hit," and "kick." Shouting increases their participation in the game.

This game provides practice in coordinating eyes, arms, and legs. The punching bag is a roughhouse toy. It is designed to withstand a great deal

of punishment. It can serve as a warmup for the many games and activities that require tumbling and scuffling.

When the clown punching bag is blown up it will easily support the weight of a two- to three-year-old. Lay it on the floor and hold its head down. Say to the children, "Does anybody want to ride a horse?"

Have the children mount the punching bag like a horse. Describe what they are doing. For example, say, "Whoa, easy old Ben. Bobby is getting up on your back," as the child mounts. To the child, you can say, "That's-a-boy. Up you go. Now you're on the horsey's back." Have the child say "giddy-up" when he wants to go and "whoa" when he wants to stop. This gives him control over the punching bag. Rock the bag back and forth to give the effect of riding. More than one child can ride the clown at the same time.

As the punching bag rocks back and forth, the children may slide off its back or side. This adds excitement to the game as long as the clown is rocking gently and there is not much chance of the children hurting themselves. After a while, you can let the children play with the punching bag without your help.

This is another game that involves shouting, cheering, and yelling.

As the children grow stronger they are able to kick the clown with more force. After a while they can actually move the punching bag with the force of their kicks.

You can move to a team game, where they work together to move the clown. Make a goal line, about ten feet from the clown, and say, "Let's see how many kicks it takes to get the clown over the goal line. Jimmy, you start."

Encourage the children to cheer for each other as they take turns helping to kick the clown to the goal: "Susie, you start now! Wow! That's a good kick!" The idea here is not to compare children, but to strengthen leg muscles and teach teamwork.

WEDGE BLOCKS

There are many muscle skill games that can be played with wedge blocks, bottlecaps, pennies, or other small objects which can be flipped or slid.

We made our wedge blocks out of scraps of two-by-fours that we found at a local lumber yard. If you have your own equipment, the blocks are a snap to make. Very often scrap material can be used as is for different games.

Balance the blocks as shown in the drawing below and then roll or slide the bottlecaps up the ramp to try to knock over the top block. This is not easy. You will have to show the child that he has to roll or slide the cap first.

Just as children kept count in the punching bag game, here, too, your child will enjoy the game more if scoring is part of it. The main way children

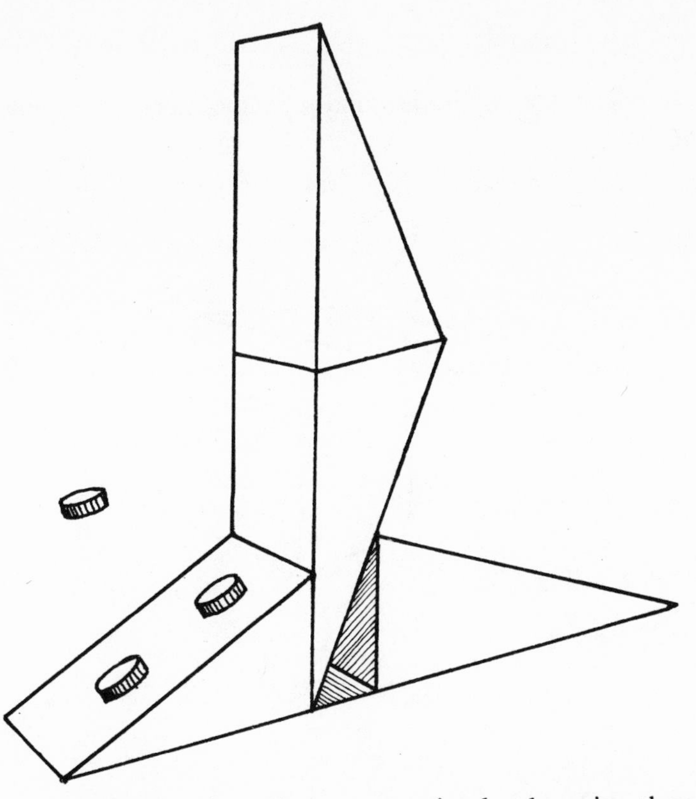

really get to know numbers is not by rote counting but by using them in action. Use "counters," not the numerals. For example, the bottlecaps themselves may be counted, or you can use toothpicks, or you can make lines on paper: ////, to stand for "four." Here again we are teaching two things at once—coordination and math. The coordination is the main aim—don't let the counting get in the way. If it helps to keep score, O.K. Otherwise, just work on muscle skill.

This is a game where you can keep score. Put the wedge blocks together so that there is a hole in the middle (as below), then try to thump or slide a bottlecap up the ramp until it falls into the hole. You can count the number of times it takes to get the cap into the hole and also keep score. Say, "I have knocked three caps into the basket and you have knocked in two." Show the child your three caps and his two.

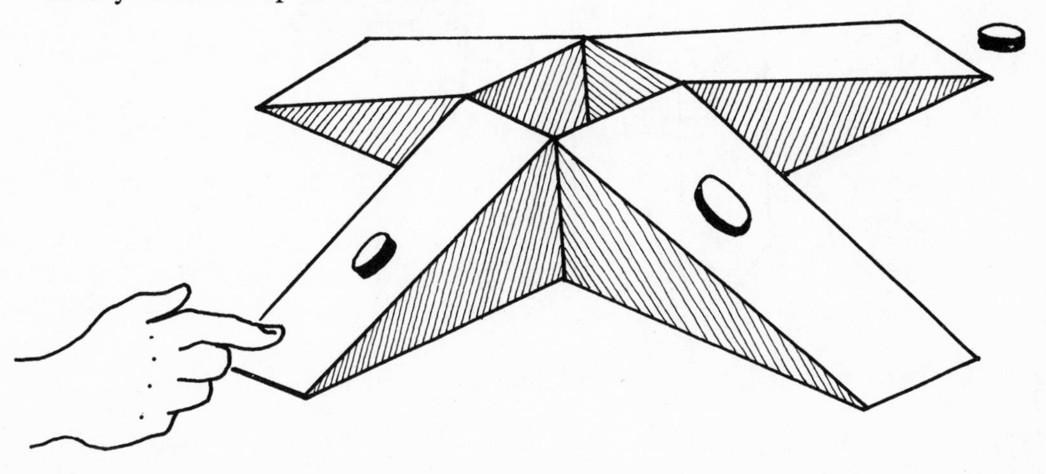

Balance one block on another and see how many caps it takes to make the block fall over.

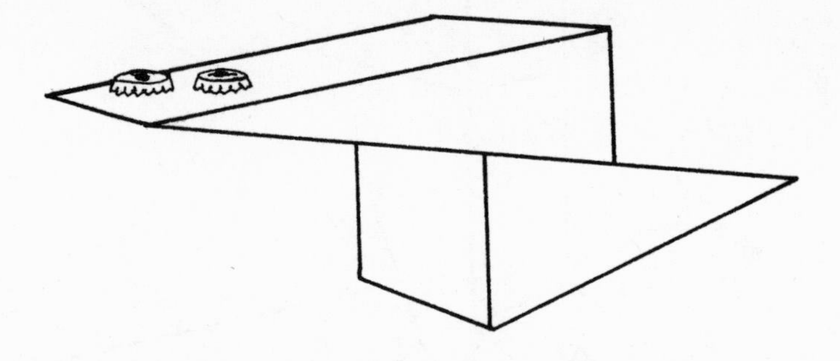

Balance one block on top of two others, as in the drawing, and try to roll bottlecaps into a can. Count how many times it takes to score a cap.

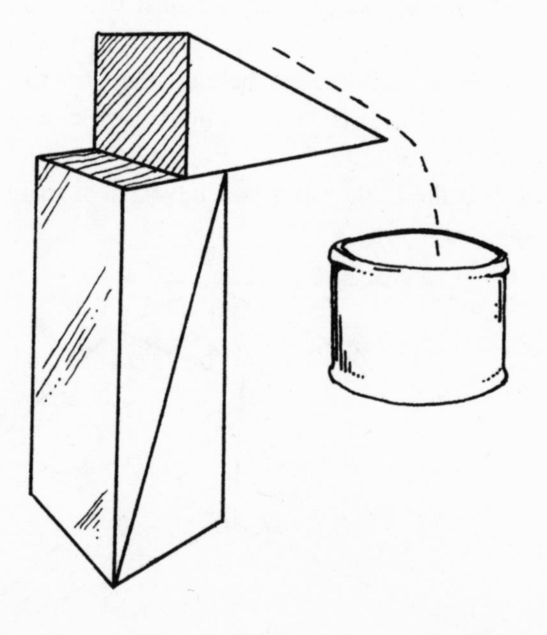

Try and roll the caps through the goal. Keep score. "I scored one. Now I have two."

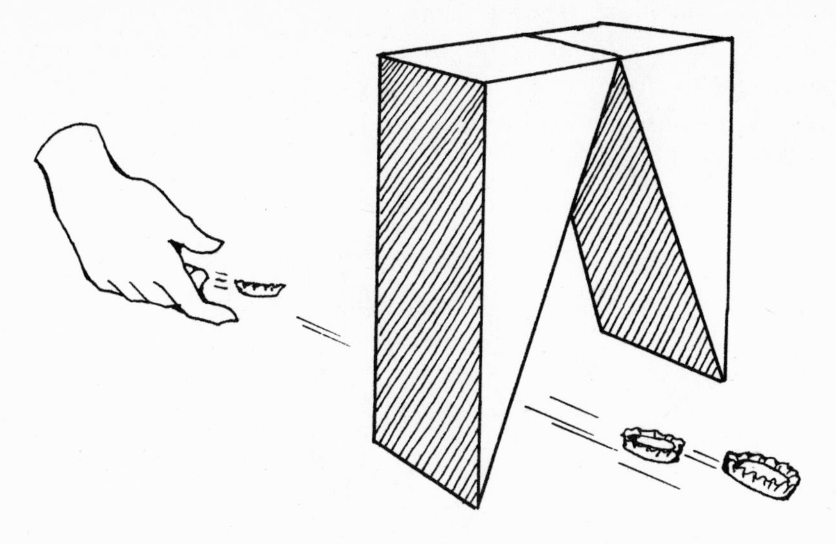

Try and roll the bottlecaps back and forth on the blocks.

Make a square in the middle of the room and throw the bottlecaps into it. Take turns and keep score.

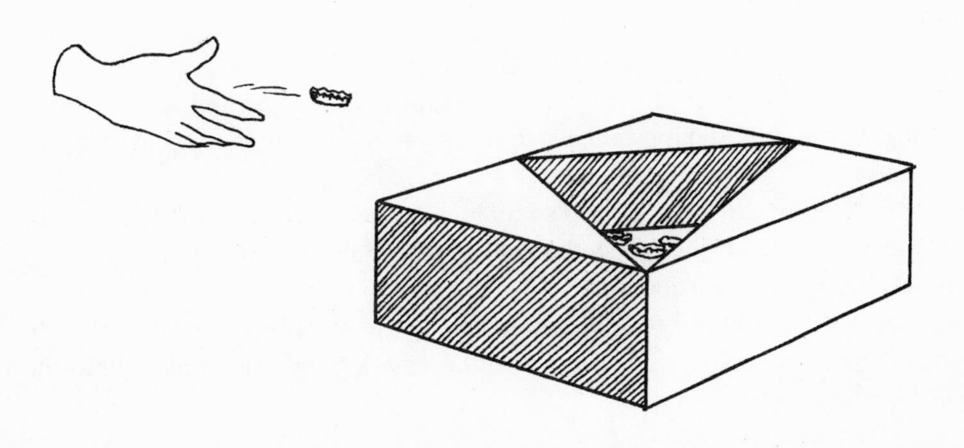

Put a penny in the top of the tepee (between the two blocks) so that it falls all the way to the bottom. Say, "Look at the penny. It fell all the way down to the bottom. Now you drop the penny and see it fall."

Vary this game by putting the blocks between you and asking him to guess which side the penny will come out: "Your side or my side? This side or that side?" Sometimes the penny stays inside. Ask, "Where is the penny? Is it stuck? Where did it go?"

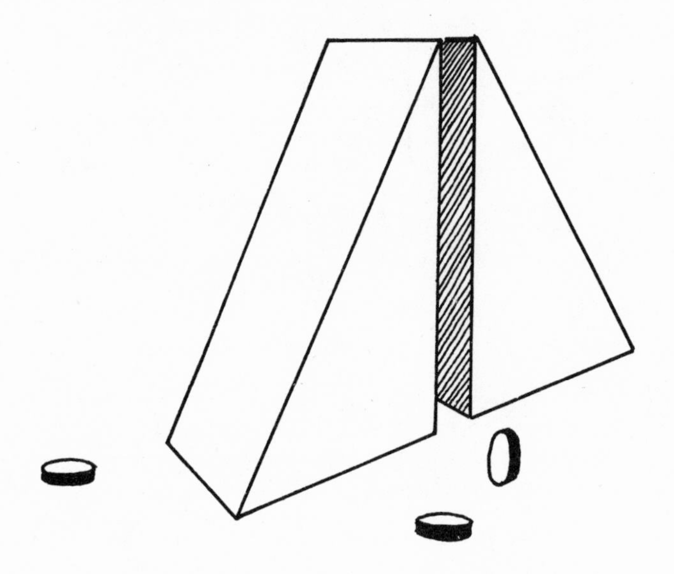

Block up one side and ask, "Which side will the penny come out now?"

Remember this is a game for both of you to play and not a test to see if your child knows the answer. Have fun!

HAMMERING

Learning to use a hammer can develop a child's later ability with tools. Playing with it and making things can influence how he uses tools for the rest of his life.

To begin, you'll need a child's hammer, some short nails with big heads, a piece of wood thick enough so the nails won't go through it, a piece of string, and several pieces of cardboard.

Tap a nail into the wood just enough so it will stand up by itself: "Watch, I'm going to start pounding the nail into the wood. Now, watch me pound the nail all the way into the wood."

Start some more nails and let the child pound them all the way down:

"O.K., it's your turn to pound. Can you pound them all the way into the wood? Try to hit the nail right in the center of the head. Good!"

A child just learning to use a hammer will have to discover where to hold his hand and arm, so that when he swings the hammer, it will hit the nail on the head. In a way, hammers and other tools are extensions of our arms and hands. Their efficient use gives us more and better ways to do things. For a young child, just the activity of pounding will be fun. Let him enjoy it. At this point, it may be the most important part of what he's learning.

After the child gets tired of just pounding, start several nails and show him how to hammer nails part of the way in. This is a good time to make him aware of the difference between "part way in" and "all the way in."

"Johnny, I've pounded this nail *all the way* into the wood, but I only pounded this nail *part of the way* in. O.K., my turn; how far do you want me to pound this nail in?" Let the child answer, then do what he wants. Next: "Your turn, Johnny, pound this nail part way in, O.K.? Right!" After the child has learned to control the hammer well enough to pound nails in part way, you can teach him how to start the nails into the wood himself. Caution: Watch the fingers! Be sure to demonstrate. "Hold the nail like this [between thumb and index finger]. Hit the nail very lightly—just a tap—so that if the nail slips, you won't hurt your fingers."

Let the child practice starting a few nails. Praise, encourage, and help him when necessary. Be patient: putting a nail into a board is a hard job which requires a lot of skill.

It's easy to make a simple pull-toy. Center a nail on one edge of a board and pound it in part way. Tie a piece of string around the nail, and you have a boat, car, sled, or whatever the child wants it to be. Additional nails pounded in part way could stand for people, animals, flags, or lights.

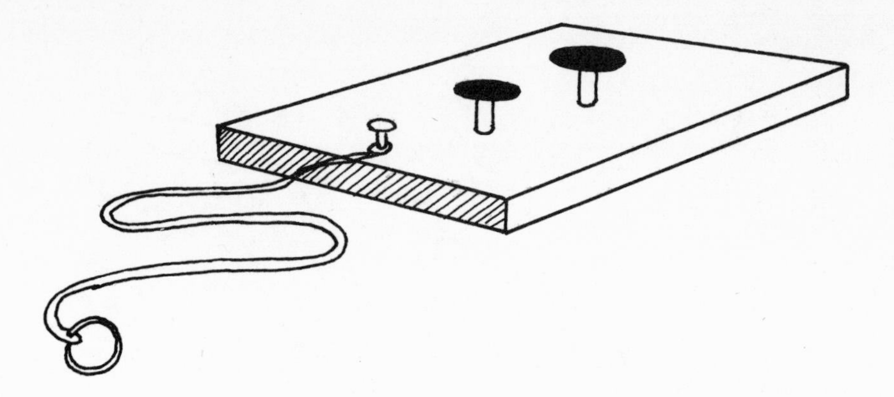

As the child's skill increases, show him how to nail two things together. It's probably best to start by nailing a piece of cardboard to the wood. By folding the cardboard in different ways, you can make a lot of different things.

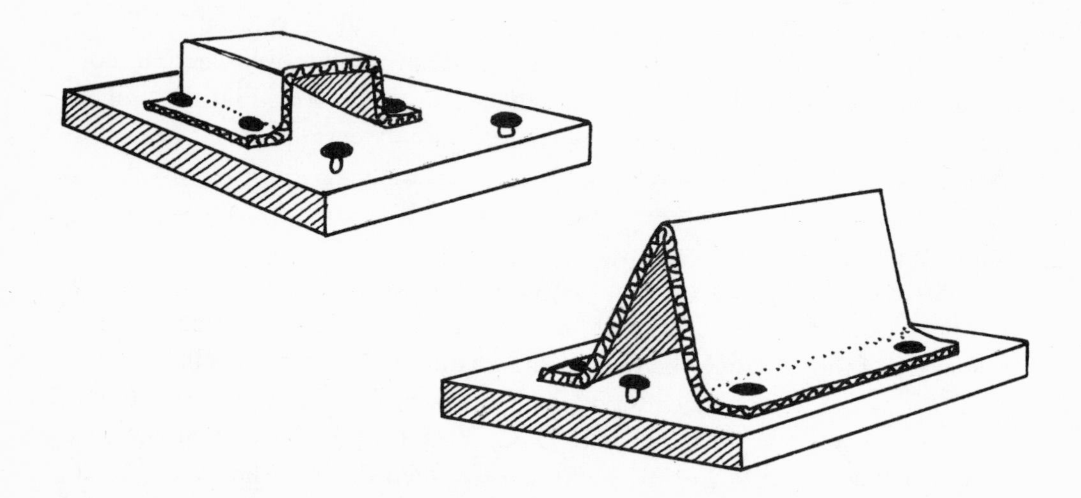

As the child tries to build different things, he'll learn what wood, cardboard, and nails are like and what can be done with them. Knowing this and being able to make things for himself will build the child's self-confidence as well as improve his skill with tools.

Caution: Put the hammer in a safe place after the child has finished playing with it. Don't let him use it when you're not around.

PICK UP STICKS

Hammering gave the child one experience in using tools; this game gives him a different kind. He has to use very careful control of his hands and fingers to succeed at this game. When you play it with him, don't be so good that he gets discouraged. But you may be surprised. It's not that easy even for adults!

Show the child how to hold popsicle sticks, for example. Then try to pick up different things with them. Play a game to see who can pick up the most things. You can also try passing things to each other this way. It will be even more interesting if you use some things that roll, like pencils.

TOOTHPICKS AND CARDBOARD

You can play all of these games with just a few simple materials: two pieces of corrugated cardboard about one foot square, twenty or thirty *round* toothpicks, and a pin or pencil for punching holes.

Start by drawing a simple picture on the cardboard—a horse, car, shoe, circle—anything, just so it's at least six inches tall (or wide). Use a pin or pencil to punch holes outlining the shape. Make the holes about an inch apart. The holes should be small enough for the toothpicks to stick in them.

Place the toothpicks in a pile beside the cardboard. Sit down with the child and start putting the toothpicks into the holes. Encourage the child to help you. If he hesitates, gently show him how to do it. Talk to the child as you are placing the toothpicks in the holes: "See, I'm putting the toothpick in the hole. Now it's your turn. Look how you've put it right into the hole. Feel how sharp the toothpicks are. Look, we're making a duck [or whatever the object may be] with our toothpicks. Here's a toothpick for you to put in. Good! Let's put toothpicks in all the holes now." Encourage the child to pick up one toothpick at a time.

You might make some bigger holes along the outside of the board which can be used as "practice" holes. If your child has trouble, you can help him by guiding his hand and showing him how to drop the toothpicks into the bigger holes. These may be big enough for the toothpick to go all the way through, and he can enjoy a separate little game of watching the toothpick come out the bottom. Another way to give him practice is by dropping toothpicks through a drinking straw. Since the hole is bigger, this will be easier, but still fun: "Watch for the toothpick to come out the other end." After the child gets pretty good at these games, try the smaller holes again.

Children also like to take the toothpicks out, so give the child a chance to do that and talk about it.

Another variation is to let the child punch the holes in the beginning.

Develop a design as you stick the toothpicks into blank cardboard. Then let the child make his own design. It doesn't have to look like anything in particular: it can be any arrangement that the child likes. You can also take turns, both of you pushing in toothpicks.

IMAGINATIVE PLAY

Through adult eyes, "child's play"—such as talking to dolls or pushing a toy truck around the floor with "brmm, brmm" sounds—is seen as a delightful but not necessarily useful activity. Dress-up and make-believe are seen the same way.

From the child's point of view, however, these are very important times. Some very necessary learning takes place during this play. A child has to get an idea of who he is—how he fits into his family and the world of people around him. He has to begin to learn that he is different from his parents, relatives, and friends. He begins to sort out the jobs he sees people do around him, both in the home and in the neighborhood.

An important part of the child's learning about himself and other people is the fact that he doesn't always (and shouldn't!) get his own way. Limits are placed on him both by his parents and caretakers ("No, no," "Don't touch," "Not now,") and by his own lack of ability. The child has to learn to handle his feelings of anger and annoyance, fear and rage. Imaginative play is his way of doing two things at the same time: learning about himself and others, and handling the feelings that go along with this. Does this have to be taught, or do children do it naturally? There is evidence that children will play a lot on their own—when the way has been prepared by their parents. The purpose of this section is to help you start the child off by pretending with him and by providing the type of toys that make it easy to pretend. You will notice how language and thought are mixed together with feelings. The young child uses language in this type of play to act out and understand different roles —such as being Daddy or Mommy. The first games are purposely contrived, but as your child grows, you should step out of it more and more, leaving the child to play either by himself or with other children. Since this play helps him deal with his feelings about *you,* you've got to be out of the way sometimes!

PICTURE CARDS

The picture cards we've used before can also be used as a beginning "let's pretend" game between you and your child. He can use the cards as though the pictures were real. The card with the picture of the dog, for example, can be made to behave like a real dog. You can pick up the dog card and make believe the dog on it is barking, or you can have it lick your face or walk around. The child can make the dog take a nap or eat. When he does this, he may talk to the dog in ways that sound like *you* talking to *him!*

That's part of the purpose—so he can handle your suggestions by giving suggestions to the make-believe dog. You may learn how you sound!

After he's done this, show the child he can pretend with the set of picture cards. Make up a simple story together about the dog and the boy and the mother. You hold two of the cards; let the child hold one. For example, hold the cards with the pictures of the mother and the boy on them. Then say, "Look, the boy is walking over to tell the mother something. 'Mommy, I found a dog. Look.' "

Ask the child to pretend he's the dog and go, "bow-wow, bow-wow."

"See, mommy, here's the dog. Can I keep him?"

"Yes, you can, but you'll have to take care of him all by yourself."

It may be helpful to give names to the picture cards. You can let the child do this. The child may also like to have the boy chase the dog.

You can probably think of some other pretend games with these cards. Use them in any way that gets the child interested, involved, and talking about them, since that is the aim of this activity.

SOCK PUPPETS

Children love to play with puppets. A puppet can be used in many imaginative ways. Puppets are especially good for encouraging children to talk and deal with emotion. Here are some easy directions for making a puppet out of an old sock. You can make the puppet yourself, or you can let the child help you. Materials are an old sock, some scraps of bright colored cloth, and a needle and thread.

Start out by putting one hand into the sock. With your other hand, push the toe part of the sock between thumb and index finger.

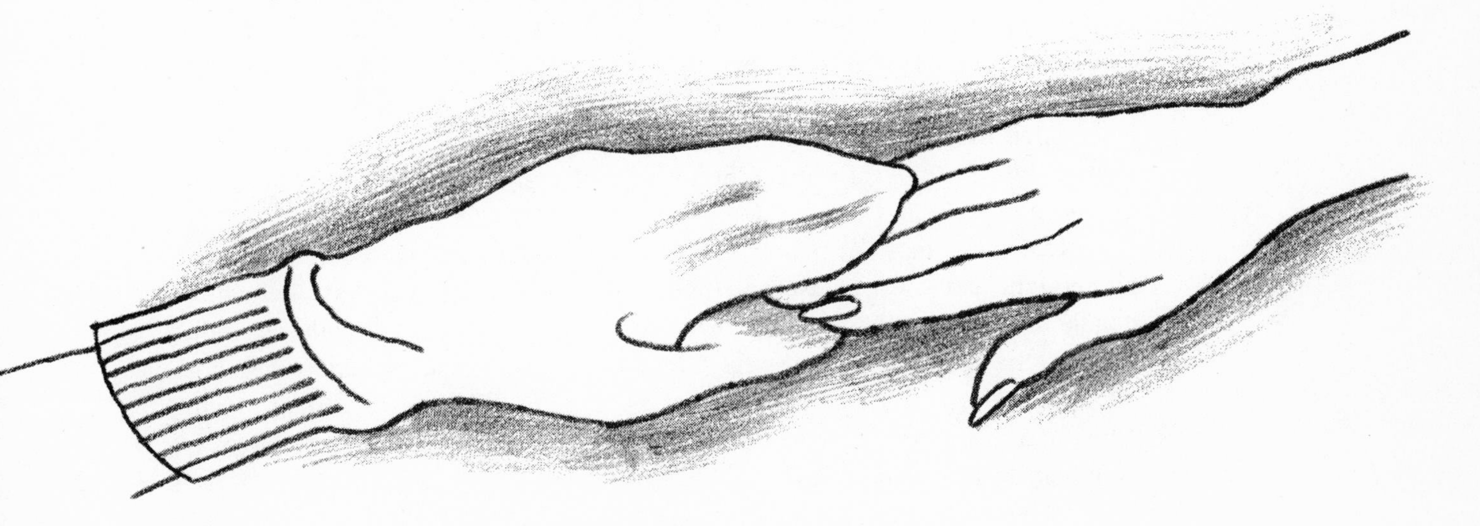

Next, sew in the pushed-in part to hold it in place. This will be the puppet's mouth. You can sew in a tongue if you wish. Cut your scraps into shapes for the puppet's nose and eyes. Sew these in place. If you want to really be fancy, you can add "ears" or fringe.

Now you should have an attractive puppet.

Before you try to play any special games with the puppet, let the child look it over and play with it by himself for a while. Sometimes children are afraid of puppets, so give him time to get acquainted with it.

At first you will probably work the puppet yourself since most young children have trouble coordinating their hands to move it. However, you can encourage the child to do this even if it isn't a perfect performance.

You and your child can act out many things with the puppet. You can make him a funny or silly puppet, or a smart one who teaches the child the names of things.

When the child seems comfortable with the puppet, give it a name. Encourage him to think of a name himself, since you want this puppet to be all his own.

Remember that the main purpose here is to encourage the child to put his thoughts into words. He will find that words, used this way, help him handle his feelings. If the puppet becomes a "real" person, the child can talk to it and make up his own answers. He can have the puppet do things he's not allowed to do, and scold it. If he sees puppets on TV, his own puppet can allow him to imitate what he's seen. He can learn much more from his own play than from watching TV.

To begin, you can make the puppet very hungry and ask the child to feed him: "Oh, I'm so hungry. I really need some food. Please, can you find something for me to eat?" The child can "feed" the puppet small blocks or crayons as food. You can encourage conversation by asking the child what the food is, whether the puppet likes it, and so on.

You can make the puppet a ball player and encourage the child to play with him: "I love to play ball. How about playing a game of catch with me?" Toss the ball back and forth between the puppet and the child. Get the child to talk by having the puppet himself talk a lot:

"That was a hard one."

"Let's roll one this time."

"See if you can catch a high one."

If you let the puppet read a book with your child, you may find that he becomes the puppet's teacher—pointing out pictures and words to it.

Remember, in this area of imaginative play, your job is to help start it off. Your child can then come up with his own ways to use the puppet, and he will enjoy playing with it by himself.

STICK PUPPETS

Another easy way to develop dramatic play is to make stick puppets. Make at least two puppets so you can each have one. Draw faces that show feelings on the sticks. Show the child that one face is smiling and another face looks sad. Use a tissue to make a skirt for the puppet. Just poke the stick through the middle. Hold the puppet underneath the skirt to use it. You can

also use pipe cleaners to make arms and legs. Sometimes the child will enjoy the creative work of making these as much as playacting with them. He may end up with many puppets—perhaps with each one showing a different emotion.

TOY FURNITURE: Uses in Day Care Settings

Toy furniture sets the stage for imaginative play, where children imitate the roles of the adults around them. They can imitate the mother, the father, and perhaps the caregiver. For this, they will enjoy using chairs, tables, an ironing board (plus iron), a sink cabinet (plus toy cookware—coffeepot, cups, tea set), a stove cabinet (plus pots, pans, dish towels, and sponges), and a doll bed (plus dolls).

Play with these toys also helps children learn the names of household objects such as furniture, fixtures, and tools used in cooking and cleaning. The child also learns the names of the various jobs that have to be done around the house: cooking, cleaning, washing, dusting, and so on.

The kitchen toys provide the opportunity for two- to three-year-olds to imitate the mother in the home. It doesn't matter if the child is a boy or girl: everybody at this age likes to play with kitchen tools. Both boys and girls can learn, through play, what mothers do.

The child's other, smaller toys can be used in a toy kitchen. Modeling clay becomes homemade bread, link sausage, hot dogs, or bacon. Beads become roast beef, biscuits, carrots, or even coffee in a cup. Make sure, though, that the child does not put these objects in his mouth. Put the clay and beads in a safe place when you can't be there to watch.

It takes very little to get two- to three-year-olds playing in the kitchen. You can just say, "O.K., I'm going into the kitchen to bake a cake. Does anyone want to help? Do you want to be a baker? Who's going to wash the dishes?" When you're in the kitchen, do all of the things that have to be done to make real cake. Turn up the oven, grease the pan, pound the dough, and shape the bread. Remember that the child doesn't care if what you are using looks real. A stick from the yard or a lump of modeling clay will serve as a loaf of bread. It is the game and the playing of it that are important.

After a while, the two- to three-year-olds will play in the "kitchen" for a long time without your guidance. They will cook, clean up, wash dishes, and serve food. Occasionally, they will check to see that you are paying attention and may offer you a taste of a delicious building block.

One of the important things about the kitchen toys is the language learning that results from these games. If you describe at each step everything that you're doing or that the children are doing, they are absorbing a lot of language. Soon you may see the children talking to each other about their play.

A part of the center can be set up for other activities that go on in the home: a wash-and-iron area, a crib area, a living room. Here children can act out many roles and learn from each other.

Remember to encourage the children to talk on their own. You can have them describe what they are cooking or doing and also give the names of the toys with which they are playing.

TOY TELEPHONES

A basic way the child learns in these years is by what psychologists call roletaking or roleplaying. The child makes believe he or she is the mother or father, and imitates in word and gesture the parent's actions. Children try out all sorts of roles, built on their view of the people around them. By pretending to be somebody else, the child comes to understand people and himself. Toys, and your play with your child, can aid this type of learning. The toy telephone, for example, can be most useful in helping your child use language in his roleplaying. Many children communicate through gestures: nodding their heads, waving their hands, and so on. But over the telephone they must talk or no one will hear them.

If your child has seen you talk on a real phone, he'll easily imitate holding the phone to his ear. However, he has only heard one side of the conversation (unless you've let the child listen to the wonder of a voice coming into his ear with no one there). With the toy phone, you can begin by saying, "Let's make believe I'm calling you on the phone. Ring, ring. Now you answer. Pick up the receiver. You have to say Hello so that the other person will know you are ready to talk." If the child still doesn't start talking on her own, ask, "Who is this? Is this Angie? It is? Well, this is Susie. Do you want to go shopping today? Can you come over for me, and we can go together?" Now wait for the child to reply. Encourage her if she doesn't and praise her if she does.

In a group setting get two children talking to each other on two toy telephones. You can suggest topics for their conversations. "Why don't you call Susie and see if she wants to have some milk and cookies now?" After a while, it might be fun to have the children call some prearranged number on a real telephone.

The toy telephone can also serve the purpose of getting children to learn to speak in firm, clear voices—a skill that will be demanded of them once they reach school. It will also help build up the child's confidence in his speaking ability.

TRANSPORTATION TOYS

The young child not only "tries on" the action of other people in his roletaking: he also acts out the scenes which surround him. Since we live in a transportation-minded world, he is fascinated not only with the real thing—such as rides in cars and buses—but also with transportation toys. They lend themselves naturally to the type of play which helps him figure out, on a reduced scale, what he sees around him on a large scale. You can help by getting on the floor and playing with him. You need to forget your adult inhibitions; sprawl out, and enjoy the actions with him. Remember, although it's a *learning* game, the emphasis is on *game*.

Two- to three-year-olds seem to like large cars and trucks better than small ones. A truck about eight to ten inches long and four inches high is big enough to carry a number of things and still small enough to be handled by a two- to three-year-old. Although children will play with little cars and trucks, most of the time they become cargo for the big trucks.

If you set up an imaginary game, the child will join in. For example, say, "Let's haul all of the concrete over to the shopping center so they can start building." Then have the child load up, with your help, a carload, truckload, planeload, or whatever he wants of blocks or beads, and haul them over to the "shopping center," stopping for all the red lights and being careful to stay within the speed limit. Your imagination is important here.

These toys offer many opportunities for talking with the child. You can teach him about policemen, firemen, mailmen, trainmen, pilots, and taxi drivers by making up imaginary games with cars and trucks. Explain things as you go along.

You can play cops and robbers. "Let's get in the police car and go catch the robbers. There they go in that green car. Uh oh, they ran through the red light. But we're policemen, so we don't have to stop for the red light when we're chasing someone if our siren is going."

Or make up a game about a taxi driver. Say, "Are you the one who ordered the taxi? O.K., get into the back seat. Where do you want to go? The grocery store? Here we go. What are you going to buy at the store? Oh, some apples and candy bars. That sounds good. Milk, too?" Continue this kind of story game with the children. Encourage them to talk. Include as many new words and ideas as you think the children can handle. Through such games children learn about their world and the people in it.

DOLLS

Dolls and doll beds offer the chance for two- to three-year-olds to imitate dressing the baby, rocking it, and putting it to bed. They can make up the bed, fold the sheets, have washday, and act out daily events. Contrary to what we thought when we were children, dolls are not just for girls, and transportation toys are not just for boys. Since the child uses toys and play to figure out the adult world, both sexes need experiences with all types of toys. Dolls are most useful for dramatic play about daily family life, and for learning to deal with emotions.

You can teach many new words to the child while he or she is playing with dolls: for instance, the parts of the body. Say, "The doll has fingers just like you. Look: one, two, three, four, five, just like you—one, two, three, four, five. The doll has eyes, too. Where are your eyes? Good—you know where your eyes are." And so on for the arms, legs, face, nose, and ears.

You can name clothes on the doll, too. "We have to take off this dress because it is dirty and put on this fresh clean one. Can you do that? O.K., you dress the doll and I'll make up the bed."

The iron and ironing board can be used in the same way as the doll and doll bed. The child has a chance to imitate the parent and to learn new roles and words.

Dolls become objects of love for the child who will enjoy rocking baby to sleep in his arms, singing a lullaby, or "fussing over" it. Dolls also take a lot of punishment: they get scolded, hit, dropped. Both love and anger are taken out on the doll, which is a very safe object to use for learning ways to handle strong emotions. In these situations, it is best if the adult observes and does not step in to interfere or teach. What you see teaches you about your child: his thoughts and feelings. From this, you can get ideas for later use in play situations.

CREATIVE ACTIVITIES

Your child has developed basic motor skill and eye-hand coordination. He has worked with blocks, paper, and other objects around the home. Now he is ready to stretch his imagination and skill in making things. Children this age enjoy what Gardner Murphy, a famous psychologist, called "messing and manipulating." They like to see what happens as they smear paint on paper, draw lines with crayons and pencils, cut with scissors, paste scraps, work with clay and things with empty boxes. This chance to be an artist of sorts is vital to a full and rich development. Too soon, people will try to make them draw cows that look like cows, make straight lines, or produce something teacher wants. In these years, the child should be able to paint, draw, build, and model with clay in ways that fit his view of the world. Skill will come, but joy of discovery comes first. The child, *if you work with him patiently,* will *want* to develop skill. He'll want to cut properly, get a crayon to go where he wants, get the sand or clay to look like what he'd like it to be.

You should try to make things, too—if you've never finger-painted or crayoned or messed with clay except in school, you've missed something! Try these activities with your child. On some he will need your help. On all, let yourself go! The last two activities in this section are mostly for you, because of the skill required. But think of how much your child might do as part of them.

As he grows older, involve him more and more in decisions about decorating or fixing up his room—and the other rooms. Let him actually help do the work. A preschooler can pick out a picture he'd like on his wall—cut from a magazine, or bought in a store. He can help put it up with Scotch tape, or hammer in the hook. Art and music are important parts of life, and feelings for them start young.

FINGER PAINTS

Finger paints are messy, but they offer the opportunity to learn colors and the experience of playing with different textures. Protect the child's clothing with an old apron or blouse, or a man's old shirt. Make sure that the paper is big enough for large movements and a lot of paint. Cover up the rug or floor so that the paint spilled won't hurt it.

Now you're ready to let the children start painting. One of the things you can do—besides standing out of the way—is to name the colors: "Jimmy is painting a big blue picture with a little red up in that corner. That's good, Jimmy." You can also point out how colors mix to form new colors: "When the red mixes with the blue it turns purple."

Don't ask a child if his picture is "real." Let him enjoy the motions of painting and the mixing of colors. If he names or describes his picture, follow up on what he says. Join in and paint a picture! The children will enjoy seeing you share their activity (and you'll like it, too)!

Remember that when you're talking to children, pointing out facts and naming things, they are learning. It may seem as if they don't understand (sometimes they don't) but they are learning nevertheless.

CLAY, SAND, AND MUD

Clay, sand, and mud are marvelous materials for self-expression. They give children a chance to pound, shape and reshape as they try to make different objects. They lend themselves to simple things: sand piles and castles, mud pies and canals, clay pots and pans. As the child gains skill, very fancy structures become possible—highways, forts, houses take shape. These are natural materials, and children learn many ideas from their use in addition to developing creativity. They learn some basic science, such as what water does to sand, and that regardless of the shape it's in, the amount of clay stays the same and can usually be put back in its original form. This may seem obvious to you, but it's an important discovery for your child, and one that can be learned only by many different experiences with these materials.

Your child will also enjoy combining materials. He can use clay and popsicle sticks or toothpicks to make "people," using the clay for the body and head, the sticks for arms and legs. He can also see ways to break the clay into pieces, as in these pictures of a man, a dog, and a nest with eggs.

As in all other games, this is more fun if you enjoy it, too. Why don't you see what you can make?

CRAYONS AND PAPER

Coloring with crayons is fascinating to children of all ages. There's hardly any need to instruct the child in the use of crayons. Just give him the paper and the crayons and let him go at it. Using crayons develops the skills needed later on in writing, drawing, and lettering.

Encourage the child to draw. It doesn't matter if the drawings resemble familiar objects. Just give him the paper and crayons and let him play.

Another use for the drawing is to help the child recognize his name in writing. After the child has drawn something, take great care to write his name on it and, if possible, display it on the wall. Say, "Bobby has drawn a good picture. Let's put his name on it and put it on the wall. B-o-b-b-y spells Bobby. There. Now we'll tape it to the wall."

PAPER PLATE MASKS

All you need to make a mask from a paper plate is the plate, a pair of scissors, and some crayons. Draw in the eyes and ask the child what is missing. If he knows, have him show you where to draw it in. If he doesn't know, then ask, "Where is the nose?" or "Where shall we put the mouth?" Draw it in. You can help the child by pointing out the features on his own face and your face, too.

After the mask is drawn, cut out the eyes, nose, and mouth. Then give the mask to the child and let him color it any way he wants.

You can finish off the mask by gluing a popsicle stick on as a handle or by tying a string to the mask so that it fits over the child's head.

PENCILS AND PAPER

Many children, even as young as a year or so, start to hold pencils as if they were going to mark on paper. Now you can take advantage of this ability. They also start to show a preference for one hand over the other. Notice which hand the child prefers. If the child seems to use both hands equally well, or has no preference, don't force him into using one hand over the other. For example, don't put a pencil or a crayon into the child's right hand to make sure that he's righthanded. Let the child pick up the pencil or crayon on his own and decide which hand he's going to use.

Of course he won't hold the pencil or crayon as you do. He may grab it as if he's going to stab the paper rather than write on it. By using his whole hand instead of just his fingers, he doesn't have to use his small muscles that aren't as well developed as the large ones in his arms. At first he may just push the pencil weakly around the paper and show little interest in what he's doing. Help him learn how to use the pencil and paper by scribbling on the page with him. Talk to him about what you're doing. Say, "I'm going to make long straight lines back and forth and back and forth." The child may watch this passively, but in time he, too, will scribble more freely and more deliberately. Soon he'll enjoy scribbling straight lines back and forth across the page with great vigor. In fact, he may not even notice that the paper ends, and he may be quite content to scribble all over the table. The only solution to this is to use bigger paper. To keep him from scribbling all over the walls, watch his adventures with the crayons until he learns what can't be scribbled on. One alternative is to make sure he has some special place where he's allowed to scribble on anything he pleases.

After the child has learned how to make back-and-forth lines, make an up-and-down line and see if he can imitate you. Sit across the table from the child, place your pencil on the paper, and say, "I'm going to make a line up and down the paper. Watch this." Push your pencil straight up the page toward the child and ask the child to do the same toward you. The child's up-and-down line may not be exactly up-and-down; it may be at an angle, it may wiggle, or it may end up as a scribble. But after a while his lines will improve.

It's also fun to associate some sound or word with the movement of the pencil. For example, as the pencil goes up the page, you can say, "Zip." The child will then say, "Zip," as he moves the pencil up the page. You will find this adds more fun to the game for him.

The next project is to draw a horizontal line. Children find this a little more difficult than the up-and-down scribble. You can either sit across from the child or next to him to draw these lines. Remember to talk about what is happening: "Johnny, watch how I'm going to make this line. Zoom! Can you make a line like that?"

The next step is to make a circle, for children also make circular scribbles about this age. Draw a circle over and over in the same place and say, "I'm making a circle. Look how it goes: around and around and around and around. Can you do the same? Let's see you do it." Again the child may not be able to copy what you have done. The circles he makes probably won't be continuous circles, but just circular scribbles. However, the object is not to get him to reproduce what you've done but to imitate your actions. In making circular scribbles he is imitating your motion.

Eventually you can lead him to the more difficult task of drawing a circle. To help him do this, place his hand in yours and draw a few circles. Then let him try by himself. Encourage him. Say, "Good! You made a real circle!"

Other shapes—such as a square, a triangle, a diamond, a square with a cross in it, or a ladder—are much more difficult for young children to copy. You can try them, but most children can't copy these until they're much older.

After the child gets used to using paper and pencil, you and he can make different things. Here are two suggested projects with paper and pencil.

In the first project, the outline of the child's hand is drawn on a piece of paper. The child may not be able to do this, so you may have to do the tracing. Or the child may be able to trace your hand. You should not forget to tell the child what is happening.

Take a sheet of paper about eight inches by eleven inches and say to the child, "Come, see how I can make a picture of my hand." Place your left hand (if you're righthanded) on the paper, with fingers stretched apart. Draw an outline with a pencil. Say to the child, "You try. Here, take the pencil and make a picture of my hand." Then move to tracing one of his hands. He'll need help because it will be hard for him to keep his hand steady while drawing the outline.

After the hand has been traced, the outline can be turned into a turkey. Tilt the paper so the thumb is uppermost. Add a beak, a wing, an eye, and feet, and the turkey appears.

After you or he has traced his hand, one of you can do yours. Then you'll have two different-sized turkeys. The little one can be the baby turkey; the big one, the mother or father turkey.

You might want to cut out turkeys and use them as a basis for making up stories. "Daddy Turkey, Mommy Turkey, and Baby Turkey are going for a walk."

For the second project you will need a piece of paper large enough for the child to lie down on. You can trace around the body or have another child do it.

After the figure has been traced, the details can be drawn in with pencil or crayon. Don't forget to draw a happy face.

The child now has a lifesize picture of himself. He'll probably want to save this. If you can, put it up on a wall with Scotch tape or tacks.

In a group situation, children can outline each other's bodies using crayons or large pencils. They can talk about body features—long or short hair, eye color, skin color, etc. Children will learn how people can look different but still have many things in common.

SCISSORS AND PASTE

There are many reasons for teaching a child to use scissors and paste. First is the pride of making something with his own hands and sharing the making with an adult. When a child sees himself as the creator of an object, he will gain more confidence in his ability to create and produce other "projects" in the future. He also gains other benefits. His small muscles develop through practice with the scissors. He'll also learn new words—words that describe and show action.

A child only two years old can learn to use scissors with the help of an adult. Some of the things that he can make are paper chains, pictures made with scraps of paper, jars made from scraps of paper, faces pasted on paper plates, Halloween costumes, and fringes for pictures.

A note about safety: Always use scissors with blunt ends. For the safety of furniture and other things within reach, make sure that the child only uses the scissors while an adult or older child watches, until you are sure he knows what he can and can't cut.

Buy a good pair of scissors. Nothing will frustrate a child more than a pair of scissors that won't cut a piece of paper or open and close easily.

There are four steps in teaching a child to use scissors.

The first step is to have the child hold the scissors with two hands and with one quick stroke cut an object like a straw while it is held by someone else. If you don't have a straw, thick paper or folded thin paper can be used. Children have great fun chopping the paper in pieces or chopping the top off a straw and watching it flutter to the ground. Make a game out of it. Have him cut on command. Say, "Ready to cut? O.K.—cut!" Laugh and comment on his cutting, as by saying, "Oh! That did it! Look at it drift down. Down it goes! Let's try another one—ready? Cut!" Enjoy it with him. Don't worry about how he holds the scissors, as long as he can't get hurt.

The second step is to cut through a wider piece of paper. This means that the child not only has to close the scissors to cut, but also must open them again, push them forward into the paper, and close them again. You'll have to show the child how to reopen the scissors and push them forward. Have him hold the paper for you while you cut. Tell him what you are doing: "See, I opened them and pushed in, and then closed them. Now you try." The child still won't be able to cut on a straight line, but he'll have learned that wider pieces of paper can be cut by the scissors. Try out different sizes of pieces of paper. Take some thin strips, about an inch wide, and some wider ones, over four inches wide. To cut thinner pieces of paper, he'll only need to close the scissors and open them again more and more.

Point out to him the wider the paper, the more work it takes to cut it. Again, how he cuts is not important; he may even tear it part way. The idea here is for the child to see that there is a connection between the size of the scissors, sizes of the paper, and number of times he has to cut. This teaches him to compare through actual work, which is the best way for him to learn.

The third step is the most difficult for many children. This requires using one hand to open and close the scissors. Look at how you hold the scissors. Some people use their thumb and the middle finger; others use their thumb and index finger. The child will learn from copying you, so use your hand the way you want him to use his. Check to see if your child is righthanded or lefthanded. If he does not favor one hand he can learn with either.

It will take him some time to learn this step. How long depends upon how well his small muscles are developed. Show him and help him, but let him go back to two hands if he wants. He will want to try your way as soon as he can, because he wants to copy you, but forcing won't help. He will be more interested in getting the paper cut than in how he cuts it.

Use such words with him as "hand," "fingers," "hold," "left," and "right." Use them in sentences describing what you're doing. Remember, his language development is part of every activity, even here.

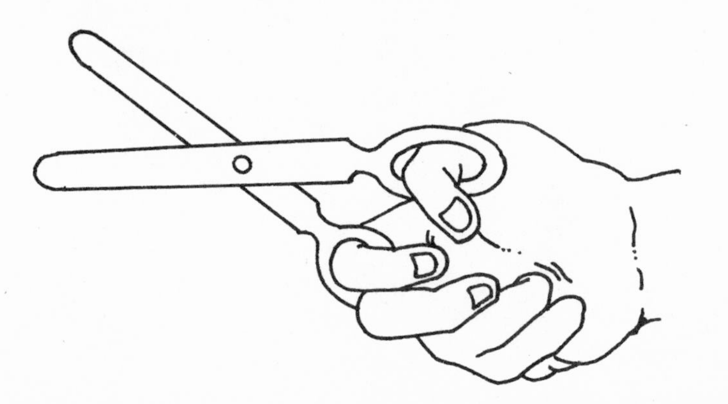

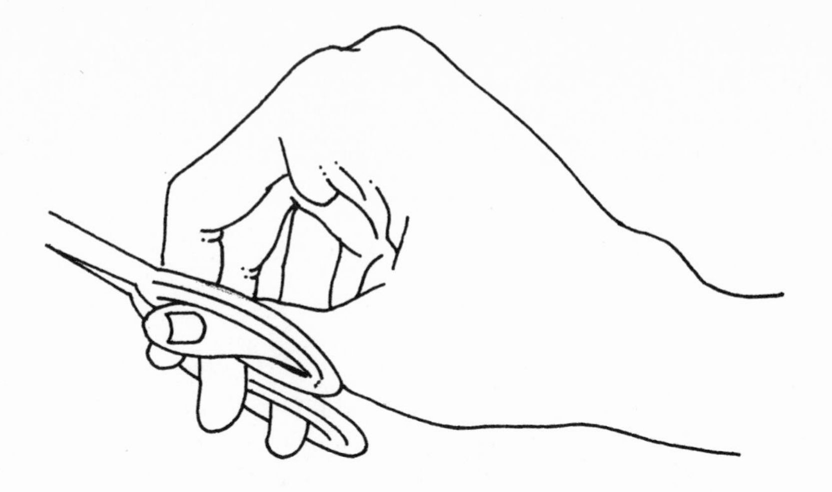

The fourth and last step is to learn to cut along a line with one hand. If he can, let him draw the line that he is to follow. This is a very difficult skill, demanding great control of the arm and hand. He has to plan ahead to see which way the scissors will be going as he closes them. Even many adults have difficulty doing this. It will take him a long time to master this skill, but it is good to start teaching him early. Remember, however, that it does take a great deal of time for most children to learn all four steps. He may be well past three years old before he can cut with one hand. He may want to practice twohanded cutting for many months. He will show you, by how he follows your actions and directions, when he is ready to move to the next step.

Here are some of the things the child can do with scissors and paste.

Scrap Paper Pictures

With the scraps of paper that the child has cut off with the scissors, you can make a scrap paper picture. As the child cuts the paper, let them drop on to a bigger piece of paper. Once there is a good supply of scrap paper, you can give him some paste and allow him to paste the scraps on the larger paper any way he wants.

He may only want to play with the paste at first, and may not understand that the paste will cause the paper scraps to stick. He may only want to paste one or two strips down and ignore the rest. If this is his introduction to paste, let him explore how the paste feels. Ask him, "How does it feel when it's still wet?" Use such words as "sticky," "gluey," "gummy." "How does it feel as it starts to dry? Does it make your fingers feel tight?" Don't be too concerned if he seems more interested in playing with the paste than in pasting up a picture. Join him and get your fingers pasty, too. Let him see you think it's fun.

When he does get some of the scraps mounted on the bigger piece of paper (and he eventually will), hang up his work of art on the wall. Freezer tape may work better than Scotch tape, because it doesn't leave marks on the wall. If you prefer, tape or paste it to the refrigerator. Show him you're proud of his work.

If you have or are working with other children, you may want to say something to the other members of the family or the other children about the picture. Make sure everybody has a chance to make a fuss over it. If you're working in a center, the work of all the children should be displayed.

Chains

Paper chains are fun to make and make great decorations. You will need construction paper of different colors to make pretty chains. The simplest way to make the chain is to cut a piece of paper about six inches wide and fold it several times. Then hold the folded strips for the child to cut with one try into inchwide strips.

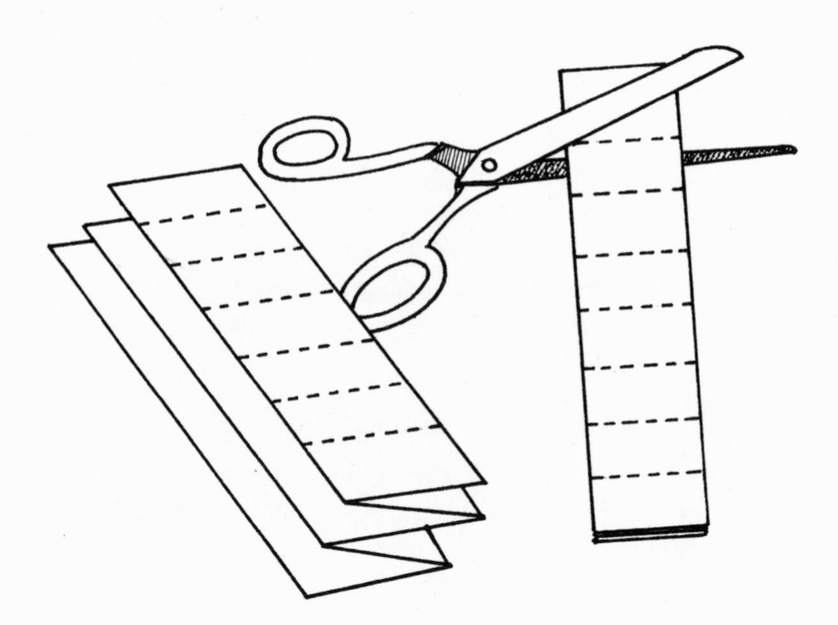

When the strips are unfolded, the paper is about one inch wide and six inches long and is ready to be made into a link of a chain. The child can put a dab of paste on the end of each strip. (A stapler can be used here also.) Most children need help to put the chain together, and so the adult may have to slip the paper through the last link made to make the new link.

If the child is good with the scissors, he can cut along lines drawn on the paper to make the links of the chain.

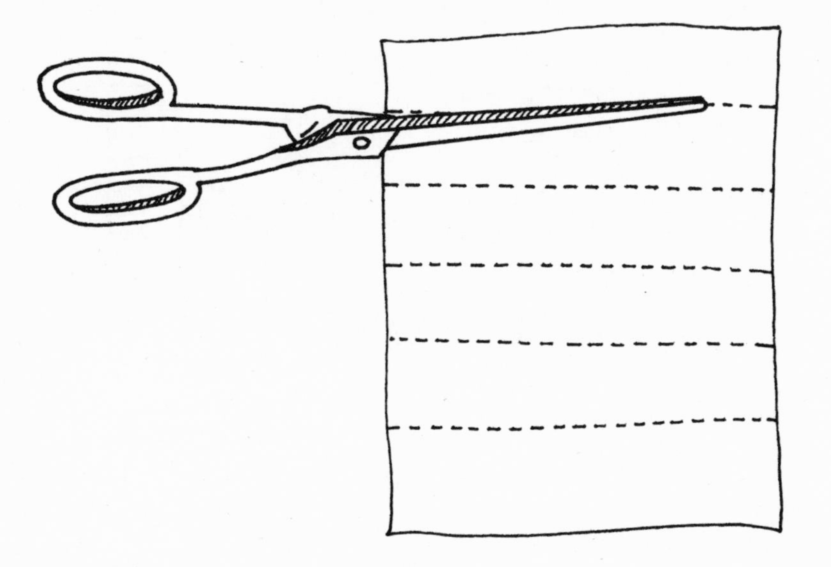

When the chain is finished, it can serve as a necklace for a child.

Fringe Benefits

You can help the child learn to cut with scissors by making a fringe for a picture. Make sure you have strips of paper wider than the scissors the child is using. You can hold the strip of paper. Show the child how to make one cut in the strip that will not cut the paper in two. Then let him cut the strip. Hold the paper in your hand and say to the child, "Cut the paper so we can make a fringe." Then move your fingers along the strip of paper and ask the child to cut again: "Cut another one right next to the last one."

Four fringe strips are needed to make the border to the picture. One long strip of paper can be cut in four separate pieces, or four different strips can be used.

After the fringes have been made, the child can paste them around the picture. One of the child's scrap paper pictures can be used, or any picture that the child likes. The adult can say, "Let's put paste on the back of the fringe and put it on the edge of the picture. That really makes your picture look pretty."

Jars

Strips of paper can be pasted around a jar by the child to make it colorful. You will need a jar or can, scissors, paper of different colors, and paste or glue. Be sure to cover the area you are working on with newspaper so that you can clean up easily.

To make the jar, fold a piece of paper several times so that it is a strip narrower than the scissor blades. Then have the child cut across the folded paper to make the strips. Again, if the child is more skilled with the scissors, he can just open the scissors and advance them through the unfolded paper. Have him cut thin strips. If necessary, draw lines for him to follow.

Perhaps he still can cut only once with the scissors and doesn't understand opening the scissors and moving them forward. This is O.K.; maybe he can help in other ways, such as by folding the paper.

Let the child do as much of the project as possible—it's his project, not yours. Don't forget that the way the final product looks is not as important as what the child learns from making it. If he produces a messy jar with some strips of paper stuck here and there, this is all a part of learning, and the child had fun making it. Any way you can get the child to help aids his development and builds his confidence.

How do you help a child complete a project (because the child *does* need help) without doing it all yourself? In this case as we have said, he can help fold or cut the paper. Start out by saying, "We're going to make this jar pretty by putting colored pieces of paper on it. When we're done you can put things in it, like your marbles or bottlecaps. Now help me cut the paper.

"Let's see if you can help me fold the paper first. Watch how I do it. I bend the paper and then I press down so it is flat again.

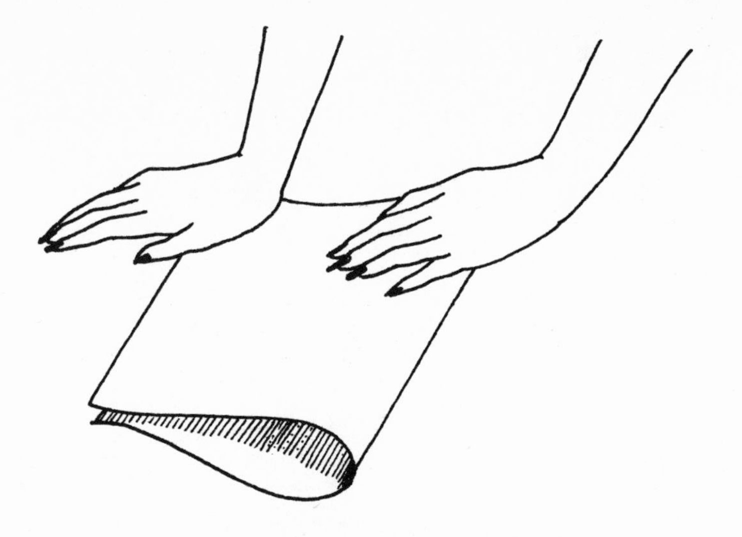

"Now you try it. I'll bend the paper and you help fold it. I'll hold your hand to show you just how to do it." Keep doing this until the paper has been folded over several times.

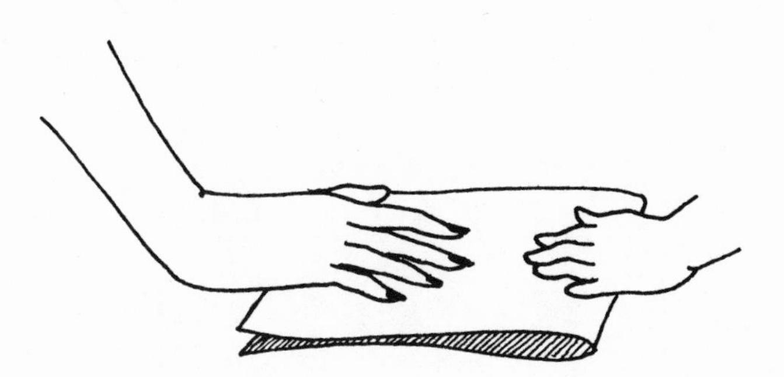

"Now we're ready to cut."

You can see how the adult is teaching the child by showing him and helping him as he makes the jar. The child does something, no matter how small, even if the adult has to help the child by moving his hand for him.

You can help the child put glue on the strips of paper in the same way. Hold the paper strips down and say, "You put the glue on the paper while I hold the paper down."

When all the strips have been pasted around the jar, the child can use it to put small things in. Pictured below are two jars children made. It's obvious which jar the child did most of the work on and which the adult did most of the work on. The child who worked on the first jar probably had no fun doing it. The child who worked on the second jar, however, probably had much fun and learned more, too.

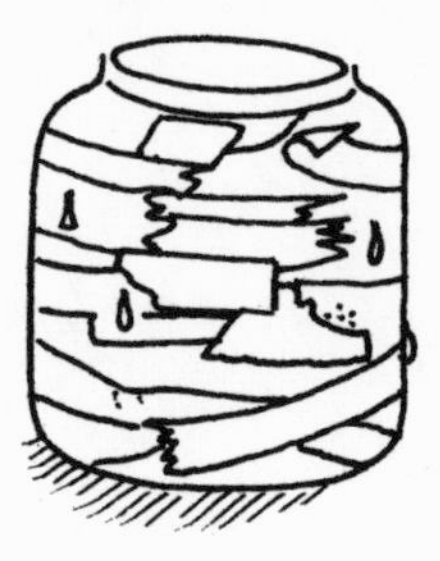

Paper Lanterns

This project is a little more difficult for a child than making a jar because it demands more cutting skill. You will need scissors, paste or Scotch tape, and a piece of construction paper about eight inches by twelve inches.

First, fold the paper in half, the long way. The child can help here as he did in the last project. You can bend the paper and match up the corners, and the child can press down to make the crease.

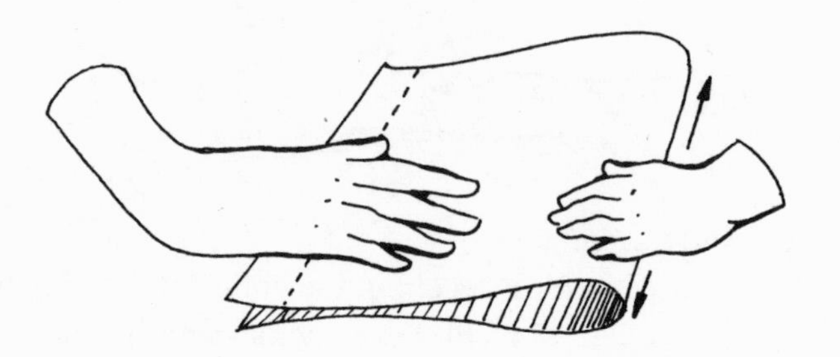

Next, draw a line an inch from the long, unfolded side of the paper. Show the child how to cut from the folded edge up to the line and stop. Make several cuts about an inch apart. Say, "See how I cut the paper and stop at the line? Now you try it."

Give the child the scissors. Help him put the scissors in his hand if necessary. Hold the paper for him with the folded edge toward him. Say, "Cut the paper, and stop at the line." Move the paper along as he cuts. If he mistakenly cuts all the way through, tape it back together with Scotch tape.

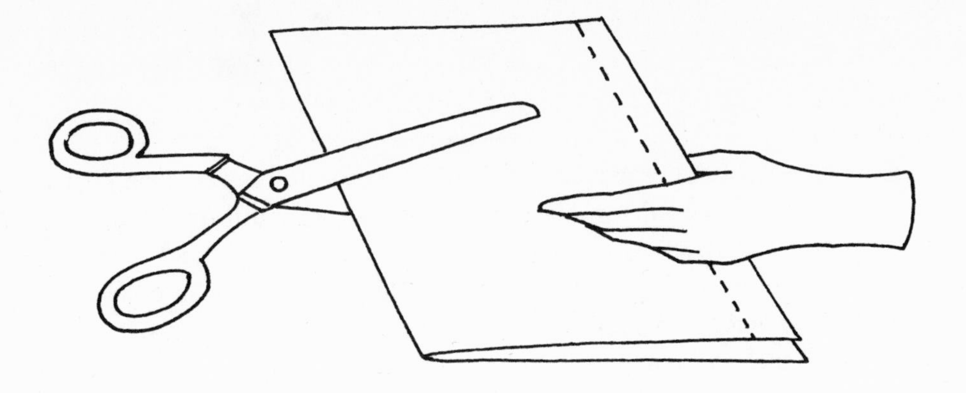

After he has made all the cuts, the lantern will begin to take shape. The adult can say, "Let's put some paste on the ends so that they can be pasted together." Tape or a staple will also work. Have the child stick the unfolded edges together to complete the lantern. Next, put a strip of paper on top of the lantern for a handle.

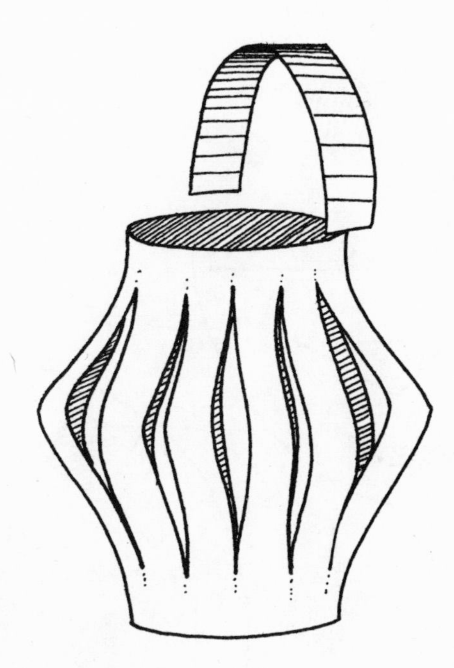

Show the child how to hold it and how springy it is. It isn't a real lantern, but it's fun for the child to make.

Scrap Paper Face

After cutting up lots of paper, the scraps can be put together to make a face. Use a large piece of paper to put the scraps on. Cut a large circle from the paper. More scraps may be needed if none of the pieces is shaped like a nose or mouth. If so, have the child cut more pieces.

Show the child the circle and say, "We're going to make a face, just like the face you see in the mirror. We're going to put a mouth on the picture, a nose on the picture, eyes on the picture, ears on the picture, and hair on the picture." Be enthusiastic about this project. This is probably the first face the child has ever made, so it's all new to him. Just where does the nose go? And what color should the hair be? If he chooses green hair, go along with it. It may look strange to you, but to him it will look fine. Give the child artistic freedom. You may find, in fact, that the first face doesn't even look like a face. The second one may not either, but the child will be learning how the features of the face are related. Soon the nose will be glued in the middle of the paper, and not where an eye should be. Look at the pictures below. They show a child's first try, and the same child's third and fifth try. Notice how he got better. He had a patient and encouraging teacher.

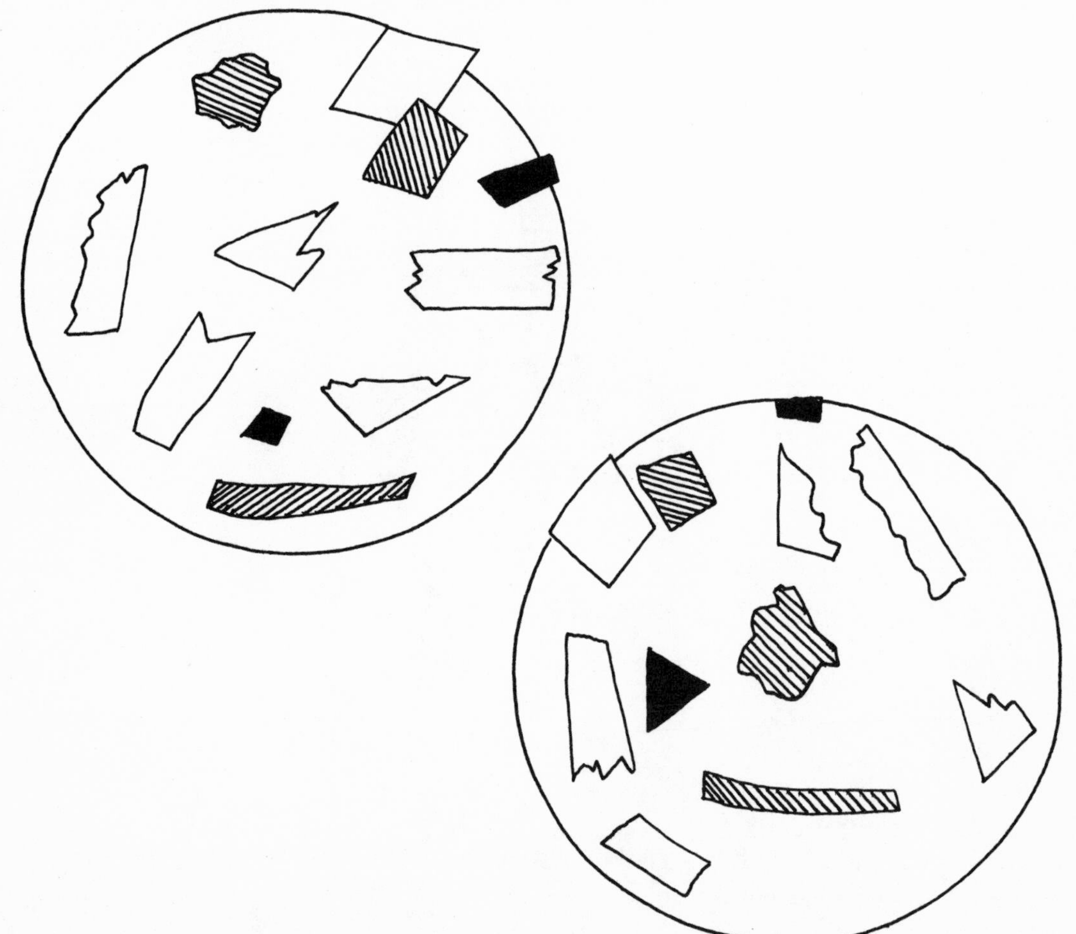

POPSICLE STICKS

You and the child will find many ways to use popsicle sticks for fun and for learning. Start out by just fooling around to see what ideas the child has. Let him use the popsicle sticks to make up games as well as make things.

Make sure you have the work space cleared so the child doesn't get confused. You may want to make all the shapes or just one at a time. Give the child some of the popsicle sticks and keep some for yourself. Show him how you make a square. Talk about what you are doing as you work: "Watch me make a square. I made a square with four sticks. Can you make a square? Here are four sticks for you." Encourage him to try by himself, but feel free to give any help he needs.

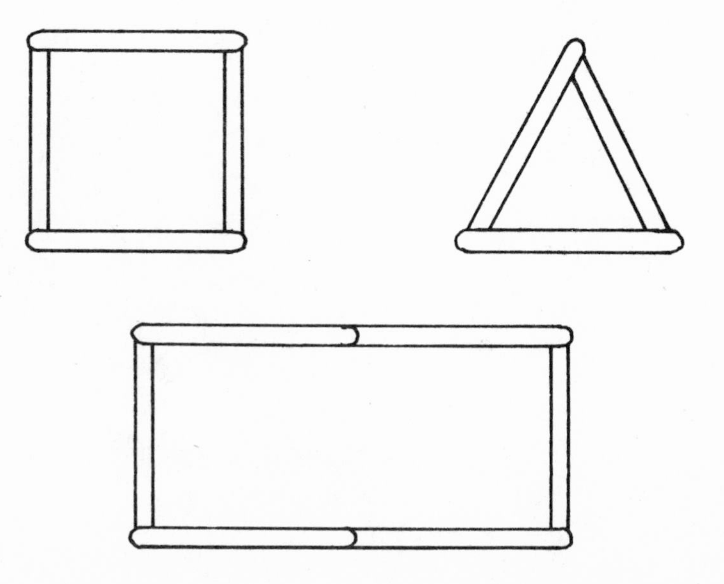

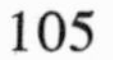

EGG CARTONS

You can use egg cartons to make toys, too.

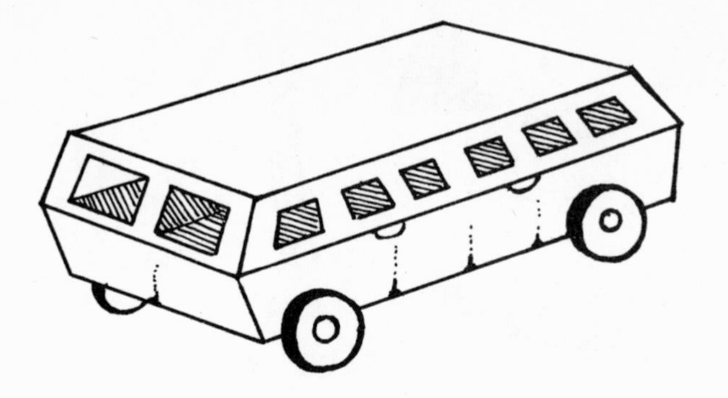

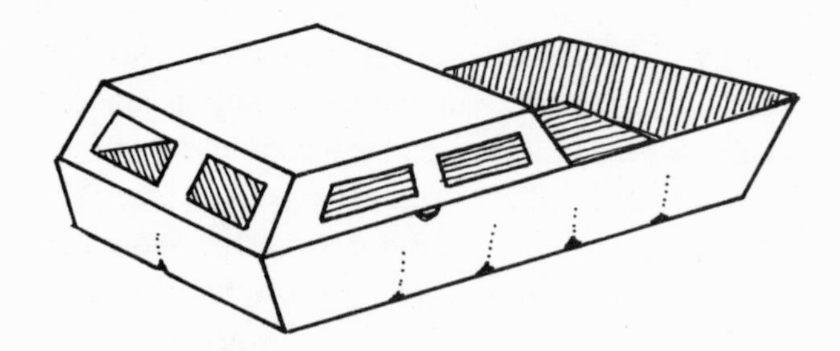

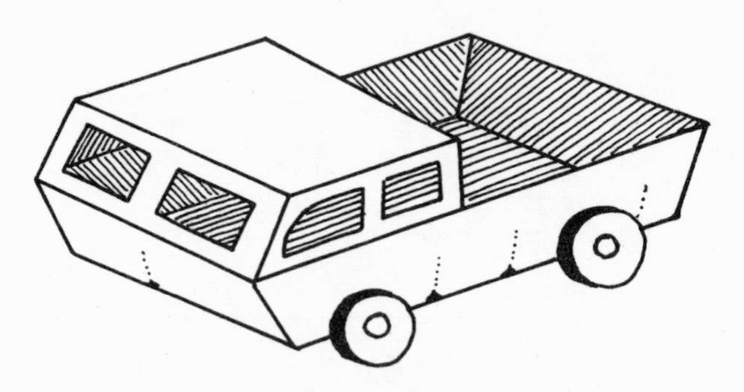

For example, you can cut wheels out of cardboard (or use Tinker Toys). Then, with a bit of imagination, you can make trucks, cars, or buses. You can also make a boat that actually floats.

WEDGE BLOCKS

All kinds of blocks are excellent for imaginative and creative play. Here are some ways we found wedge blocks to be useful tools for stimulating these types of play.

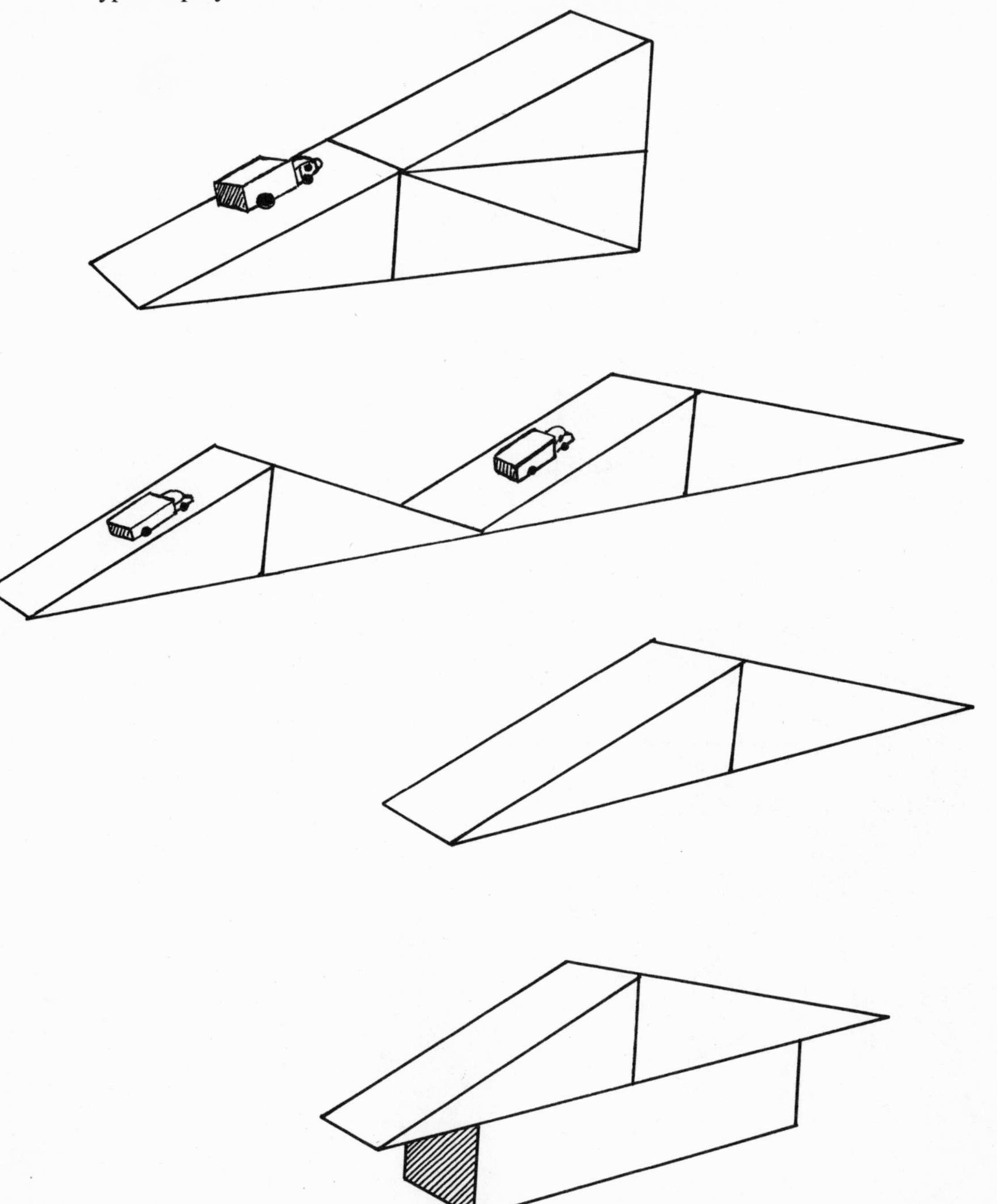

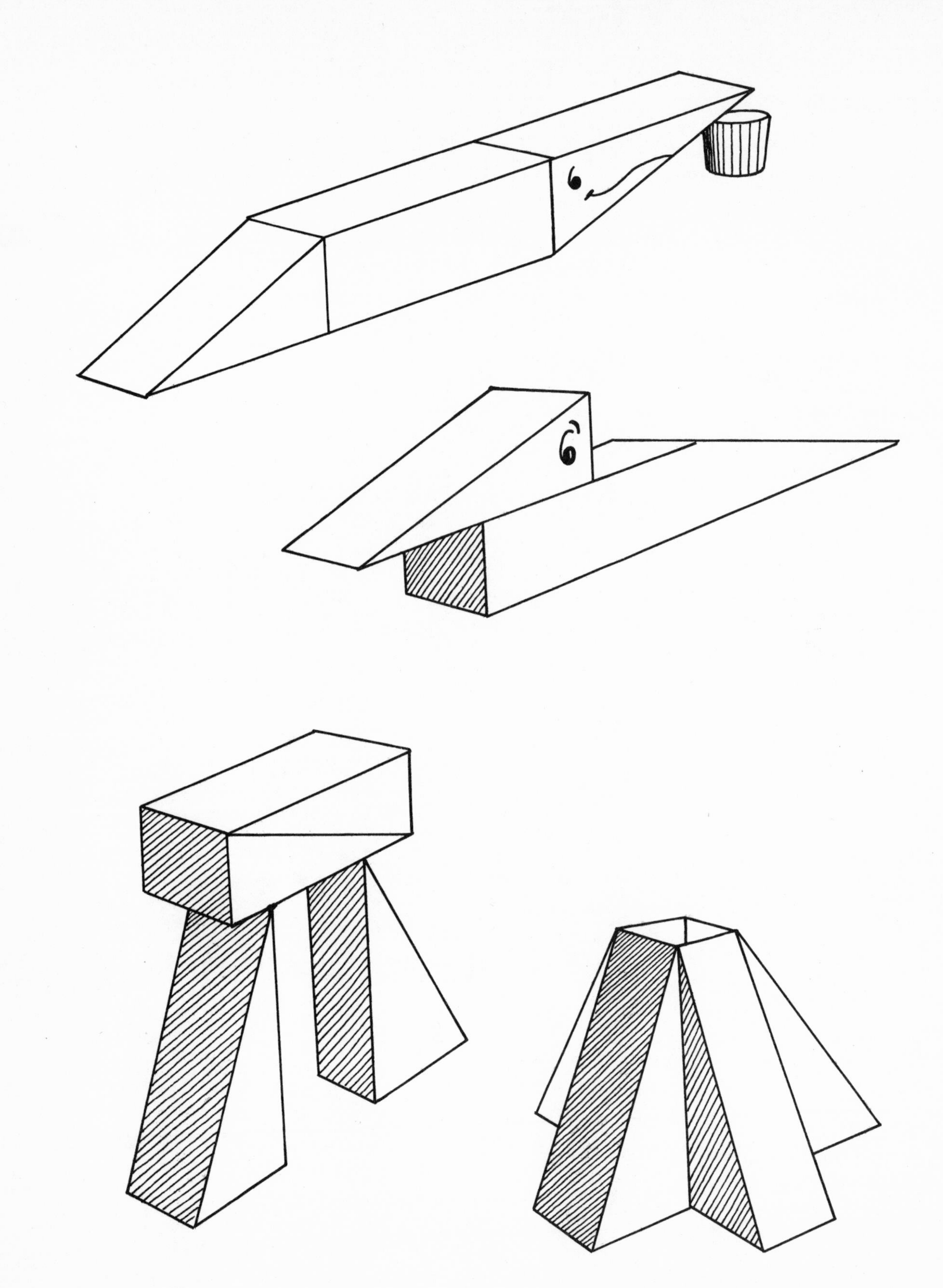

DADO BLOCKS

A new and interesting set of blocks have been recently designed, called DADO Blocks,* which allow the child to build by attaching the blocks rather than just stacking them or placing them in rows. As you can see by the picture, the blocks are thin, but have large and easy to handle notches. The child attaches two blocks by putting the notches together. The added value of these blocks is that they come in four sizes, from one notch on each side, up to four on the two long sides. The sizes are exact, so that four of the small make one of the large. That means children can have more experience with number and space as they use these blocks for creative play. The blocks are suitable for use by one child at home, or for groups of children in a center.

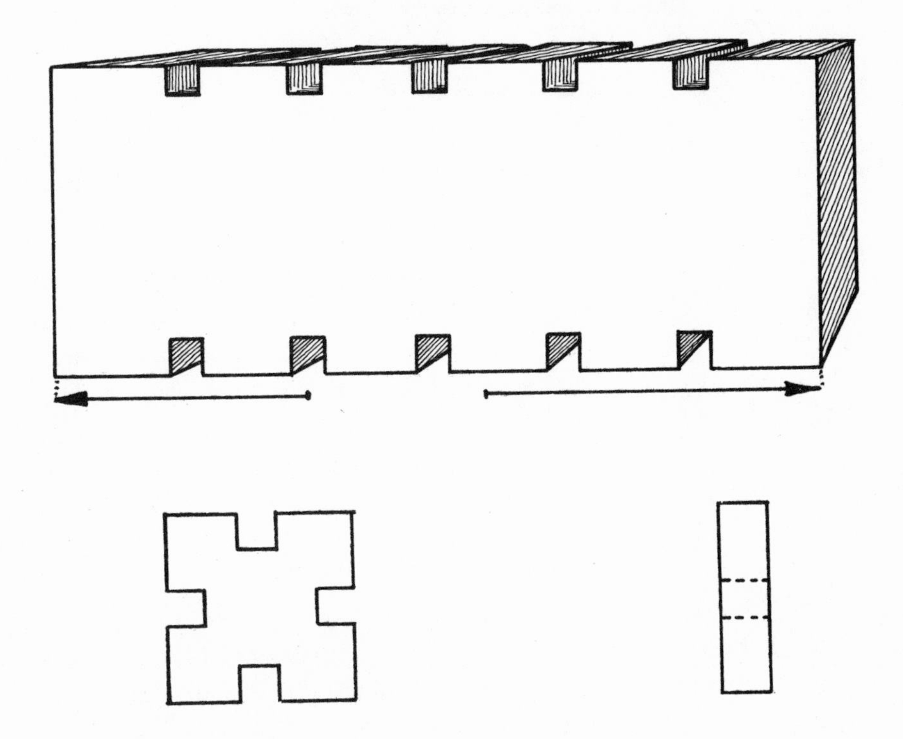

MUSICAL INSTRUMENTS

Your child has probably already discovered that cans, pans, blocks and what-have-you can be banged on the floor (or against each other) to beat out a rhythm, so probably the last thing you want him to make is a drum! How about something less noisy—like a stringed instrument?

Take a block of wood and have the child hammer a line of small nails (brads) at one end of the block. Then have him hammer some more on an angle

*Milo Products Corporation, Grantham, Pa. 17027.

to the other nails at the other end. Get some rubber bands that will fit right around the nails, and you have a simple stringed instrument—a ukulele or guitar. You'll have to plan this, and mark the wood so that rubber bands will be right. You can make one with string, too. The main idea is that when he plucks the bands, he gets a sound. We've even had preschoolers tell us that the sound depends on the length of the rubber band!

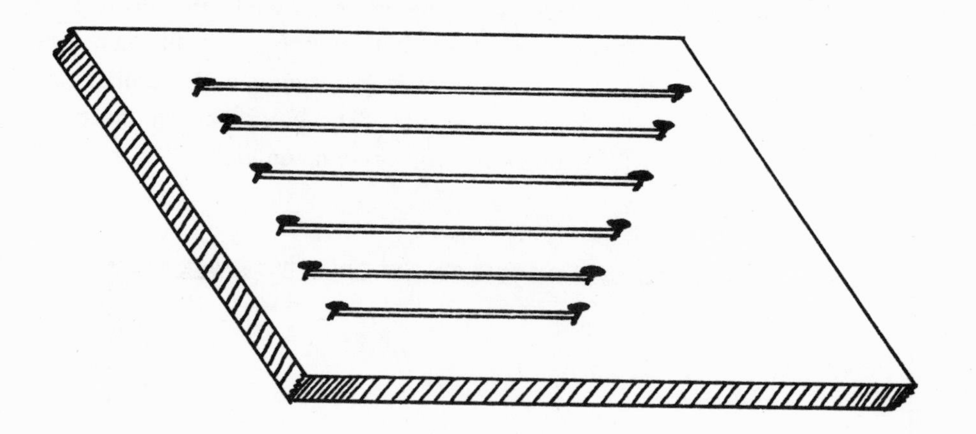

A Japanese violinist named Suzuki has developed a way to teach children as young as three years old to play the violin. He starts them out on a small one, built for their hands and arms, but one that has a good tone. They also listen on records to good violin music, so that they get the idea of a "good sound." There are Suzuki groups in the United States, and it is clear not only that children can learn, but that they like it. Being able to make music gives a child (or adult for that matter) a great sense of competence. It's something that stays with us for life, and we now know that, carefully done, it can begin early.

Some words of caution: First, don't push, or you can kill desire. Second, it might be wise to avoid cheap, toy musical instruments that can't give a proper sound. There's a difference between making a ukelele that the child knows is a toy, and playing with a poor imitation of the real thing. For example, if there's a real piano around, let the child press the keys. It shouldn't be off limits. Most parents can't teach their own children to play. You can light the flame, however, by exposing your child to song, dance, and musical instruments. And delight in their attempts to make music.

TOY BAGS

You can do many things to give the child a place to put his own things. One is a place to hang his coat, labeled with his name. Another is a locker, again labeled with his name, in which to place his crayons, drawings, and other things.

Something you and the child can make is a toy bag. An old pillowcase and a piece of string are all you need. Most pillowcases already have a hem around the open end. Just make two slits about an inch apart in the hem and feed the draw string through the holes. Your child may be able to help with the stringing.

If you can't find any old pillowcases, it is still simple to make a toy bag. You will need a piece of material about forty-eight inches long and eighteen inches wide, needle and thread, and a piece of string thirty-six to forty-eight inches long.

First, fold the cloth lengthwise and *make sure that the side that you want to show is on the inside*. Then stitch up the sides.

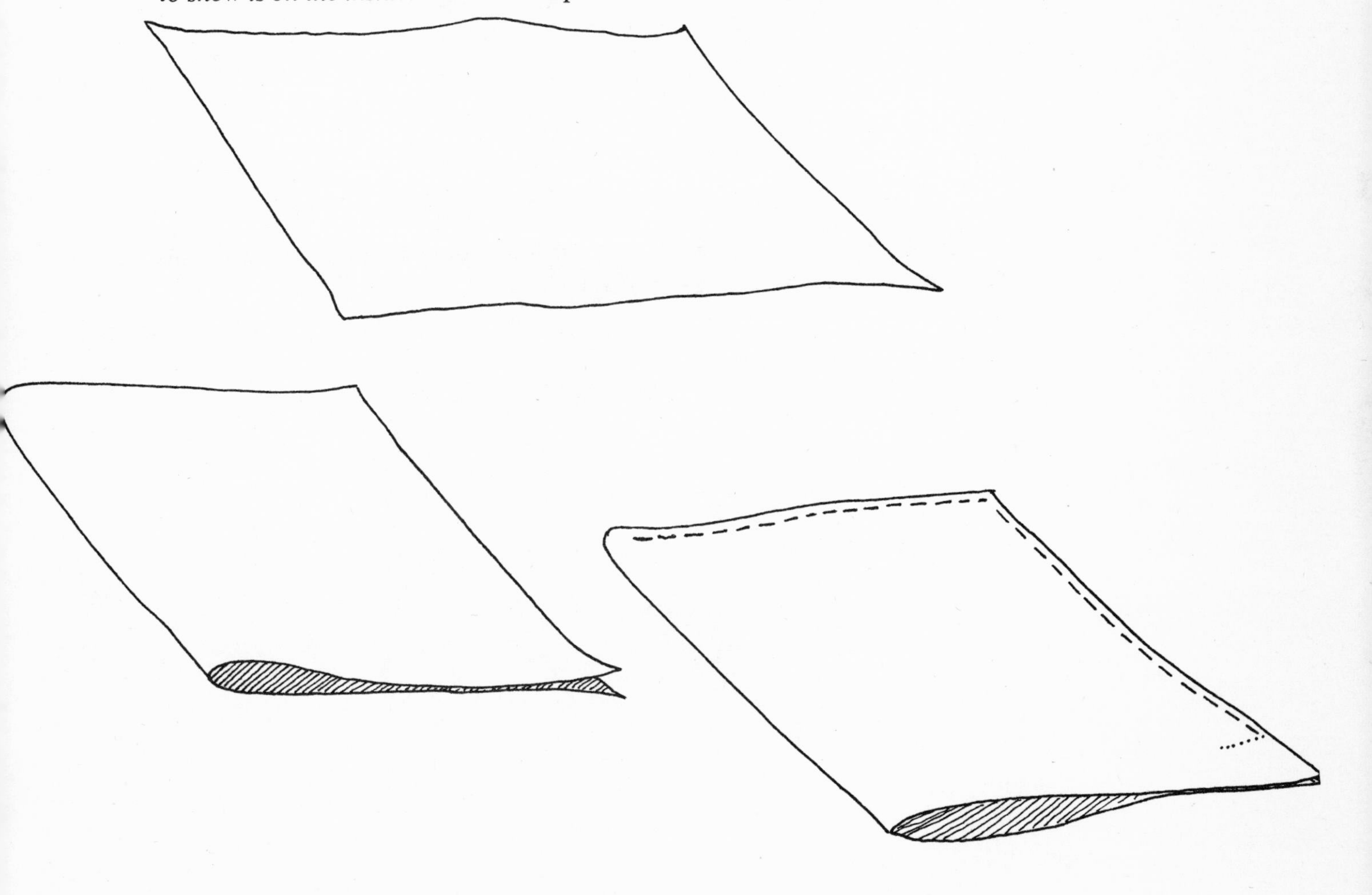

Next, make a hem for the drawstring. Fold the open edge back about one inch. Then stitch the fold down so that you leave a place through which you can run the string.

Now turn the toy bag inside out, cut two slits about an inch apart in the hem, and feed the drawstring through the holes.

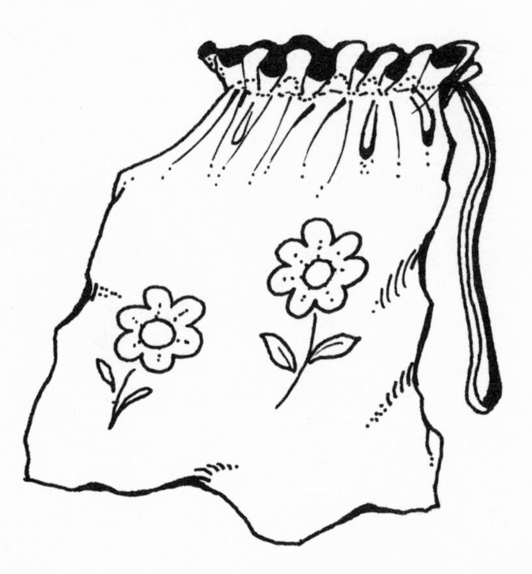

Now, the toy bag is finished. You can decorate it if you wish. Be sure to put the child's name on his toy bag. If he wants to decorate it himself, all the better.

HALLOWEEN COSTUMES

A Halloween costume can be made from a large paper bag from the grocery store. The costume won't last very long, but that isn't too important, since most of the fun is in the making.

Materials needed are a large paper bag, construction paper or Halloween pictures, crayons, scissors, and—to make the costume extra fancy—scraps such as tin foil, string, or tissue.

First, cut out holes for the head and the arms. If the child has practiced the scissors activities, he can do the cutting. Tell him, "Here is a big bag. We can make it like a shirt for you. I have a hole in the top for your head and two holes in the side for your arms." If he is afraid, cut the paper bag down the back to help him put it on.

Let the child see himself in the mirror before you begin to work on the costume. Tell him, "All I can see are two arms, two legs, and a head. Don't you look funny?" Next, take the bag off. Use the scraps and pictures to make a costume. With a little help, the child can cut a fringe on the bottom of the bag, paste pictures and scraps on the bag, color the bag with crayons, and paste bits of strings, material, and tin foil on it. Let the child do as much of the work as possible and let him decide how he wants it to look. Halloween costumes are fun to make; in fact, you don't even have to wait for Halloween. Any time is a good time!

SOME FINAL WORDS

The purpose of this book has been to provide you with a variety of activities which can be used to extend and enlarge a child's experiences, and to contribute to his growth—both intellectual and emotional. This book of ideas is best used as a guide. The adult who plays with and sets the stage for play, is the most vital factor in the child's development.

Learning is a continuous process, and the child's later learning, based on the building blocks you've laid in using this book, still requires your involvement. The quality of the continued adult-child interaction will affect his further development. You cannot say that the job is ever finished. In the next few years, before formal school, he will need to continue the close one-to-one activity and sharing times with an adult. He will enjoy, more and more, the company of other children of various ages. His play with them will teach him vital lessons of living with others which can't be learned as well in any other way. Your role moves on from the direct, one-to-one play, to more and more teaching, by arranging for him to be with other children. Through the usual give-and-take, the occasional spat over toys, the arguments of childhood, he gets a clearer picture about himself, and acquires, in child fashion, the great realization that other people's behavior and ideas are not always like his, and that what you know depends upon your own personal experience with the world. You cannot and should not protect him from learning this lesson, even though, in learning it, he begins the long growth of moving away from adults as the center of his world.

In the next few years, his language will grow tremendously, and you will enjoy your conversations with him. If you have stimulated his mind, his curiosity and interest will range widely. It will push you to keep up with his questions. Always try to answer, even though it seems his queries are endless. He doesn't need long or fancy answers. His ability to understand the causes of things he sees is still limited, but he does need to question and to be listened and responded to.

Although his command and understanding of language will grow for the next few years, he will still be a child, and will still learn best through play and action, through dealing with real things and toys rather than through words alone. Although he will memorize words, songs, and rhymes he hears from adults, other children or even TV, being able to say the word, count to ten, or rattle off the alphabet doesn't mean he understands all he says. Words are no substitute for experience; seeing and hearing cannot replace doing and trying. Keep him, if you can, an active learner, not a passive receiver. To assist him in this active pursuit, he will need three types of games, toys, and activities. When you buy materials, seek a balance. He needs some items that he can play with by himself, some that require other children, and some that require you, or other adults, to enjoy with him. Sometimes he can use the same materials, such as a puzzle, or blocks, or a book, in all three ways. You can select on the basis of possible multiple use.

Your delight in your child will continue to grow as you observe him, play with him, watch him learn and develop. Your pride in yourself, too, will grow as you realize your active role in helping him learn.